2nd Edition

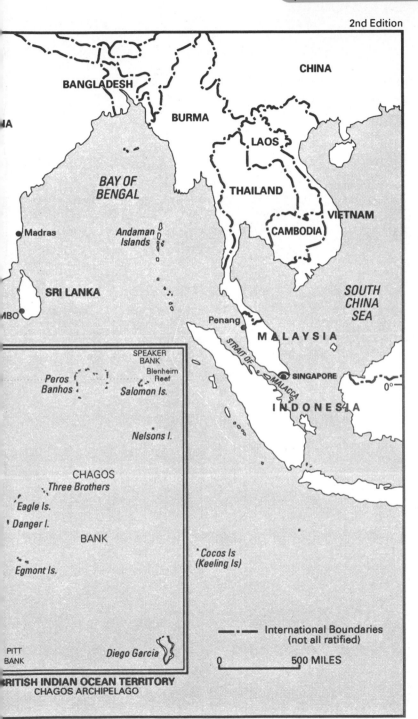

CHINA

BANGLADESH

BURMA

LAOS

IA

BAY OF
BENGAL

THAILAND

VIETNAM

CAMBODIA

Madras

Andaman
Islands

SOUTH
CHINA
SEA

SRI LANKA

MBO

Penang

MALAYSIA

SPEAKER
BANK

Blenheim
Reef

Peros
Banhos

Salomon Is.

STRAIT OF MALACCA

SINGAPORE

0°

INDONESIA

Nelsons I.

CHAGOS
Three Brothers

Eagle Is.

Danger I.

BANK

Cocos Is
(Keeling Is)

Egmont Is.

International Boundaries
(not all ratified)

PITT
BANK

Diego Garcia

0   500 MILES

BRITISH INDIAN OCEAN TERRITORY
CHAGOS ARCHIPELAGO

Foreign and Commonwealth Office Library Map Series 23 (92)

PEAK OF LIMURIA

PEAK OF LIMURIA

The Story of Diego Garcia

Foreword by
HRH the Duke of York

Richard Edis

BELLEW PUBLISHING
London

First published in Great Britain in 1993 by
Bellew Publishing Company Ltd
8 Balham Hill
London SW12 9EA

Reprinted 1994, 1998

ISBN 1 85725 070 2

Front and rear endpapers: Foreign and Commonwealth Office
Library

Designed by Mick Keates
Phototypeset by Intype, London
Printed and bound in Great Britain by
MPG Books Ltd, Bodmin, Cornwall

Acknowledgements

The author would like to acknowledge the generous help he has
received in preparing this book from the following: Fred Barnett,
Chris Bayly, David Bellamy, Barbara Bond, Charles Borman, Mervyn
Brown, Don Cairns, John Canter, Andrew Cook, Richard Cox,
William Foot, Alan Francis, David George, Fred Hatton, Tom Harris,
Martine Jardine, Kees Dirkzwager, Dan Layman, Shirley Miller,
Simon Malpas, Marcel Moulinie, David Stoddart, Bob Strike, Claude
Talbot, Nigel Taylor, John Topp, Stephen Turner, Francisco
Viqueira, Roger Wells, Elizabeth Wood and HRH the Duke of York.

Contents

I was delighted to be given the opportunity to read this excellent book about Diego Garcia by Richard Edis who was Commissioner for the British Indian Ocean Territory from 1988 until 1991. It makes fascinating reading for anyone who has sailed the Indian Ocean and especially for those who have been fortunate enough to visit the island, as I was when I was serving in HMS Edinburgh in 1988.

I can testify to the remoteness of the Chagos Archipelago and to the low profile of its coast line. When bound for Diego Garcia and after a few days at sea it is a testing moment for a young navigation officer of a warship when confirmation of the accuracy of his work is received barely an hour before the established time of arrival. The low lying terrain is never quite able to express itself as an island paradise but there are rich compensations in the abundance of marine and birdlife. And I am glad to say that the expansion of the military facilities, while adding immeasurably to the strategic role and economy of the island, has not been allowed to interfere with the precious balance of nature.

The sea and maritime affairs have always been and always will be the prime factors in shaping the island's destiny. It is now over twenty five years since the birth of the British Indian Ocean Territory and Richard Edis' eloquent account of the history of Diego Garcia is a timely and informed contribution to the island's records.

Preface

The idea for this book came to me when I was out for a run, a practice I have pursued with pleasure along jungle paths on my frequent visits to Diego Garcia. During such visits I found among the people who were working there an appetite for knowledge about the island's past, which I hope that this modest study will help to satisfy. I hope it will also serve as a souvenir of time spent there for the thousands of men and women who have lived on or visited the island. Now that the name Diego Garcia has become known internationally because of the present military facility, there may be wider interest too.

It might be assumed that, apart from the area developed as a naval facility in recent years, the Chagos Archipelago is a paradise largely untouched by human hand. While it is true that the reef and marine life surrounding the islands is uniquely rich and unspoiled, the land itself and the wildlife on it have been altered drastically by human agency over several centuries. From the dawn of the modern age the islands, and Diego Garcia in particular, have been washed by the tide of world events and touched by the ebb and flow of empires. Not surprisingly in view of their location it has been the sea, maritime expansion and naval power which have shaped the island's story, as this book will show.

Originally I had in mind only a short booklet but I soon became absorbed in the surprisingly rich amount of original material available about this small island, especially in the archives of the Foreign and Commonwealth Office and the India Office Library, and decided to produce a more comprehensive work. Essential for anyone who wants to go deeply into the history of the area as a whole is Sir Robert Scott's beautifully written book *Limuria,* which was published in 1961 in Britain and reprinted in the USA in 1974. Sadly it is now out of print but should be available in good reference libraries.

Although my book touches only briefly on natural history, the bibliography mentions several works on this subject, an appreciation of which can considerably enhance enjoyment of the island. The most comprehensive of these is *The Geography and Ecology of Diego Garcia* by Stoddart and Taylor. Although not specifically about Diego Garcia, David Bellamy's *Half of Paradise* about two scientific expeditions to other islands in the Chagos Archipelago is very readable.

This study is dedicated to all those whose lives have been touched in some way by this wonderful island. The proceeds from the sale of this book will go to the protection and promotion of Diego Garcia's natural and historical heritage.

RICHARD EDIS

June 1993

I

A Laurel on the Sea

Diego Garcia is the largest of more than 50 islands that make up the Chagos Archipelago, which constitutes the present extent of the British Indian Ocean Territory (BIOT). The Territory is the sole remaining dependency of the Crown in the region and is situated near the geographical centre of the Ocean from which it takes its name.

The Chagos Archipelago is one of the most far-flung areas of the globe outside the polar regions. Diego Garcia lies roughly 7 degrees south of the Equator and 72 degrees east of Greenwich. The Chagos are separated from the nearest land by huge expanses of ocean, 'utterly lost in the great water wastes: star land in sea space', as the writer Alan Thompson poetically described them.[1] The southernmost Maldives lie 400 miles to the north, the Cocos-Keeling islands 1500 miles to the east, the Seychelles 1000 miles to the west and Mauritius 1200 miles to the south-west. Over 2000 miles to the south lie the bleak windswept islands of Amsterdam and St Paul. All these islands are themselves outposts in the immensity of the Indian Ocean.

The remoteness of the Chagos is best appreciated when the approach is made by sea. Yachtsmen, fishermen and the crews of warships and supply vessels still make the trip.

Whether by sail or steam this involves a voyage of many days with nothing but ocean and only seabirds, dolphins and flying fish for occasional company. Another vessel is a rare sight indeed. Otherwise, there is only the long swell, the approaching squall and the theatre of sunset and sunrise to break the monotony.

A dozen or so miles from Diego Garcia a low line is scarcely discernible which gradually comes into focus as a fringe of coconut trees and a white line of breakers on the reef. From the north, the only entrance to the lagoon, Diego looks like a string of small islets, each with its crown of high trees. The scene has scarcely changed today from the sketches made by eighteenth-century naval officers to guide future mariners making their landfall. As a vessel approaches the Main Pass, it becomes apparent that there are three small islands masking the mouth of the lagoon and that what appear to be two other islands are the embracing arms of a huge atoll. The air is full of frigate birds, boobies and terns. The vast lagoon, 13 miles long by $4^{1}/_{2}$ miles across, stretches far away into the distance, forming a small inland sea, a little world turned in on itself.

Describing the scene in 1885 in terms that remain true to this day, the naturalist Gilbert Bourne said:

> On a fine day, the varied colours of the still waters of the lagoon, the low-lying strip of land covered with vegetation of a vivid green, the dazzling strip of white sand which borders the shore and the clear sunny sky, will afford a picture which will not easily be forgotten.[2]

The sea was the traditional way to approach Diego Garcia. Nowadays the more usual way is by air from the Gulf, Singapore or Mauritius. Although crossed infinitely more swiftly, the vastness and emptiness of the ocean still impress and intimidate through the aeroplane window. Massive, towering clouds make stately progress like the billowing sails of galleons. The sea below is an opaque dark blue. Suddenly there is the excitement of sighting land after many hours over nothing but water. 'A laurel on the sea, a circle of bursting, startling green', a Second World War soldier-poet described it.[3]

Indeed what the traveller notices at once from the air is the dramatic shape of the thin necklace of land, which appears little more than an outline of a pencil mark on the ocean. Of all the atolls in the Chagos Archipelago, Diego Garcia is the most perfect, forming a shaky V-shape extending about 15 miles from north to south and with a distance of about 35 miles around the circumference from tip to tip. Visitors have called forth various images to describe its shape. The early nineteenth-century Mauritian historian, Charles Grant, the Viscount of Vaux, described it as being 'in the form of a serpent bent double'.[4] The eighteenth-century French cartographer, Abbé Rochon, said more prosaically that it 'resembled a horseshoe'.[5] Its more recent, late twenti-eth-century American residents have likened it to the outline of a footprint in the sand, with the islets at the mouth of the lagoon forming the toe-marks.

From the air, the vivid contrast between the varying blues of the lagoon, lighter, and with more green, than the dark blue indigo of the surrounding ocean, is apparent. It is also possible to make out on the upper western arm of the island the wide apron of the airfield, neatly arranged low-lying buildings, antennae in extensive aerial farms, ships at anchor in the lagoon and, as the plane makes its final approach, the roofs of the old plantation buildings peeping out of the vegetation on the eastern side.

Travellers arriving today in Diego Garcia, whether by air or by sea, must first be processed by British India Ocean Territory Customs, in their smart and functional sand-coloured uniform of desert boots, long socks, shorts, shirt and beret with the Crown and palm tree badge. The red telephone box at the airport entrance is a further reminder that this is British territory. However, the drive along the fine road leading from the airport or the fleet landing jetty to the Downtown area on the north-west tip of the island is reminiscent of the Florida Keys and a reminder that the present residents are predominantly American.

The road runs through immaculately groomed grass verges, past the civilian workers' accommodation, the British Club, the sports fields and other recreational facilities, the fire station and the Cable and Wireless building with its satellite dish, to the impressive, white, headquarters building overlooking the lagoon, outside which the Union Jack and the Stars and Stripes fly side by side. Not far away stands the BIOT police station with its traditional blue British police lamp and the distinctive wavy blue and white BIOT flag flying outside.

The Downtown area, containing the quarters of the military personnel, has all the facilities of a small town, including an interdominational place of worship, shops, eating-places, a swimming pool, a bowling alley and a bus service. Everything is beautifully laid out with ample lawns and carefully planted decorative trees and shrubs. Incongruously, broods of wild chickens peck their way nonchalantly between the buildings, and the occasional feral cat is to be seen padding about. Madagascar fodies flit from tree to tree, red-capped if in mating plumage. The human residents, American, British, Filipino and Mauritian, military and civilian, male and female, make their way about on buses, bicycles and on foot, in the last case often in jogging kit. Near the northern tip is Cannon Point, where two 6-inch guns still point out to sea, as they have done since 1942.

As you drive south down the island beyond the airfield, the buildings and facilities begin to thin out. A poignant reminder of the past is the well-maintained cemetery near the old settlement of Point Marianne, containing the resting place of earlier islanders as well as graves from the Second World War. It now contains a monument to those who fell in a more recent conflict, that of the Gulf in 1991. The thick vegetation that lines the road on either side conceals the narrowness of the land and lends a deceptive air of spaciousness as the ribbon of the road unfolds. There are only occasional glimpses of the calm waters of the lagoon on the one side and the breakers on the reef on the ocean side, even though these are at some points separated by only 100 yards. Large land crabs scuttle across the road, which is scattered with the shells of those who lost the game of chicken with vehicles.

Half way down the western side, beyond the Donkey Gate, which is designed to keep the animals clear of the runway, wild donkeys, alone or in groups, begin to appear. They are especially numerous in the extensive grassland areas around the transmitter antennae near the southern bend of the island, looking for all the world like game on the African plains. Near the transmitter site is Turtle Cove, where small lemon sharks and turtles can be seen swimming in the clear water of the narrow channel leading from the lagoon to a large, enclosed, swampy area known as Barochois Sylvaine.

The road becomes unpaved coral as it leaves the area set aside for military purposes near the bottom of the eastern arm. It passes at first through fairly open coconut groves but the vegetation thickens markedly as it approaches the old plantation area at East Point.

East Point is a completely different world from the Downtown Area. Here are the remains, which the British authorities are trying hard to preserve, of a plantation society which lasted for two centuries. The manager's elegant *château*, recently restored, dominates the plantation square and faces the old jetty, cross and flagstaff by the lagoon shore. Around it stand the plantation chapel, itself also recently restored, the jail, the blacksmith's shop, the store, the hospital, copra mills and the remains of the copra drying sheds. The orange blossoms of a flame tree and pink and white ground flowers add colour to the scene. On the shore lies the remarkably intact wreck of a Second World War Catalina flying boat, still shining silvery in the sun. Farther up there is the morgue and behind it a macabre 'bleeding stone' where corpses were drained of their blood, around which the moss seems to grow with especial luxuriance. Nearby is the old graveyard with tombs from far back into the nineteenth century. The last burial, that of a small child, dates from 1971 just before the evacuation of the plantation.

Beyond East Point the road becomes no more than a track, heavily encroached on by the vegetation. After the brooding remains of the old settlement of Minni Minni, now almost lost in heavy vegetation and thick with moss and ferns, the track reaches Barton Point. This is the extreme north-east tip of the island and is a distance of about 37 miles by road from the north-west tip at Simpson Point. There is a fine beach of white sand between Barton Point and Observatory Point, studded with shells of all shapes and sizes, many of them occupied by small hermit crabs, and pieces of white, pink, green and blue coral. In the waters offshore, the coral heads of the reef are host to a myriad of fish.

Opposite Barton Point lies East Island, the largest of the islets at the mouth of the lagoon. It is designated as a nature reserve and is the home of large numbers of red-footed boobies which roost in the vegetation, and ferocious-looking giant crabs, which lurk in holes in the interior. The remains of buildings and machinery from the coaling station era are also in evidence there. Middle Island has a small interior lagoon of murky water from which you half expect some sea monster to erupt as a tidal surge makes itself felt.

Beyond the extensive reef around Middle Island, known as Spurs Reef, lies the deep-water channel of the Main Pass, on the other side of which is the small scrap of West Island and so back to Eclipse Point. There are few finer places to be on a clear, balmy night under the palm trees, the dark-blue velvet sky alight with stars, and the waves breaking translucent white in the moonlight on the reef.

II

Takamakas,
Turtles, Corals,
Coconut Crabs,
Shearwaters and
Sharks

Diego Garcia is a low-lying tropical atoll with an average elevation of only 6 feet above sea level. The maximum natural elevation is around 25 feet in dunes near Point Marianne. If the greenhouse theory of atmospheric warming with a consequent rise in sea level is valid, the Chagos group, like the neighbouring Maldives, must be one of the places in the world most vulnerable to its impact. So far, however, there is no sign of significant encroachment by the sea and indeed the land area has shown considerable stability since it was first mapped accurately more than 200 years ago.

The surface area of Diego Garcia is not much more than 10 square miles. The island is composed entirely of coral rock. Some pumice rock found near Barton Point is likely to be debris from the explosion of the Mount Krakatoa volcano in the East Indies (now Indonesia) in 1889. There is a layer

of poor soil which in places barely covers the underlying
coral but in more heavily vegetated areas has a depth of a
couple of feet of peaty earth. The typical profile across the
island starts on the ocean-side reef with a wide, eroded, sea-
washed platform of dangerously sharp rock, a scattering of
boulders and a narrow, sandy beach. There is a steep ridge
at the edge of the land which then slopes gently downward
to a less pronounced ridge and another sandy beach on the
lagoon-side. In places the land is indented on the inside rim
by depressed areas with narrow entrances which flood and
drain on each tide and are known as 'barochois'. Particularly
extensive barochois are found in the south and south-east,
such as Barochois Maurice and Barochois Sylvaine.

Diego Garcia is the wettest tropical atoll in the Indian
Ocean and experiences average rainfall of over 100 inches a
year. Gilbert Bourne, visiting in 1886 observed: 'it would be
scarcely beside the truth to say that rain may be expected
every day; that at least was my experience.'[1] If not quite true,
it is rare for there to be periods of more than a few days
without rain, which comes in short, intense downpours,
which race as squalls across the lagoon. There is consequently
a high water-table of surprisingly unbrackish water, taking
into account the proximity of the sea on every hand. The
explanation, which was discovered quite recently, is that there
are extensive 'water lenses' in Diego Garcia, caused by fresh
water, with its lower specific gravity, floating on top of the
sea water which permeates the ground at a lower level. These
fresh-water lenses are readily tapped by shallow wells. There
are few natural bodies of standing fresh water above ground
but rainwater gathers sufficiently after the frequent downpours to provide adequate drinking water for wildlife.

The climate of Diego Garcia was described by an early
visitor Charles Pridham, in 1846, in the following terms:
'there is almost continually a delightful freshness and softness
in the atmosphere, and although very hot in the sun, the air
where there exists any shade is cool and the nights invariably
very pleasant.'[2] Temperatures generally range between the
upper seventies and the mid-eighties Fahrenheit (25°–28°C).

There is a high level of humidity but it is ameliorated by frequent breezes and is less stifling and enervating than elsewhere in comparable latitudes. The island is also mercifully free of unpleasant tropical manifestations such as malaria.

There are distinct if marginal variations of season in Diego Garcia which are governed by changes in the predominant winds, which in turn govern the direction of the currents. From December to March the wind blows mainly from the north-west under the influence of the monsoon, which brings hotter temperatures (an average of 85°F/28°C) and heavier rainfall (a mean of over 12 inches in January). In April and May there is a transition in the prevailing wind from the west to the south-east. From June to September the south-east trade winds blow and the weather is cooler (79°F/26°C) and relatively drier (6 inches of rain in June). October and November is another period of transition, with variable wind directions. Diego Garcia is fortunate to lie between the northern and southern cyclone belts in the Indian Ocean, so avoiding the storms which periodically devastate Mauritius, Reunion and Rodrigues to the south and the coast of the Indian sub-continent to the north. However, the tail of a cyclone will occasionally clip the island, usually during the period of the south-east trades.

Behind the rhododendron-like 'scavvy' thicket (*Scaevola tacada*) which fringes the shores, the vegetation of the island is now dominated by coconut trees, either of self-sown 'cocos bon dieu' (God's coconuts) or the cultivated variety established in the plantation era. Early historical accounts suggest that this was not always so and that much larger areas were covered by broadleaf trees. Impressive varieties of the latter which survive individually or in clumps around the island are the white wood tree (*Hernandia sonora*), the rose or mapou tree (*Barringtonia asiatica*) and the takamaka tree (*Calophyllum inophyllum*). The white wood tree can grow to a height of 60 feet and has small, cream-coloured flowers. The rose tree is even taller and has a massive girth. It has leaves 18 inches long and its flower of four white petals, with a mass of slender pink stamens protruding from the centre, gives

off a heavy scent. The flowers last only from dusk to dawn of
a single night but when fallen they spread a fragrant carpet
round the tree. The seed husk of the rose tree has a characteristic square shape, designed, like a coconut, to be water-
borne. The takamaka grows slowly into a giant oak-shaped
tree and is supported by a widespread network of roots above
ground. It has shiny leaves with fine parallel veins, a small,
delicate flower with a clump of yellow stamens at the centre
and fruit like a large gooseberry. The wood of the takamaka
is excellent for boat-building and has been used as such
around the islands of the Indian Ocean to construct traditional craft such as pirogues.

A number of other impressive trees were introduced in
the old plantation areas, such as the giant fig trees at Point
Marianne and Minni Minni and the breadfruit trees at East
Point. It is not clear when the ironwood tree (*Casuarina*),
with its needle-like leaves and pine-like appearance, was introduced. Its seeds are very resistant to sea-water and it is possible that they arrived originally on drifting branches. However,
it is now spreading widely in the areas where construction
has taken place because of its liking for disturbed soil. Its
ability to extract and fix nitrate from the soil gives it an
advantage over other vegetation. Numerous other exotic
flora – fruit trees, shrubs, flowers, vegetables and grasses –
were introduced in the plantation era and more recently
for decorative and dietary purposes. Both the amateur and
professional botanist will find Diego Garcia a happy hunting
ground.

Diego Garcia also holds delights for the ornithologist. At
least 35 species of bird have been identified. The bird population has been subject to vicissitudes over the years. Before
the arrival of man there were probably enormous colonies
of seabirds and also possibly some native species of landbird.
Human activity had a devastating effect on the bird life. The
vegetation was, as we have seen, transformed by the cutting
down of much of the natural broadleaf woodland and its
replacement by coconut trees. Worse still, predators were
introduced in the form of rats, cats, dogs and, of course,

man himself, for whom birds were a source of meat, eggs and feathers.

The closing of the plantations and the rigorous conservation policy of the BIOT administration may well have led to a revival of a number of species which had become rare or disappeared from the island altogether. Today, long-standing winged inhabitants of Diego Garcia which can be termed indigenous include various sorts of terns, noddies, boobies, frigates and green herons. The island is also a staging post for migratory birds such as shearwaters, turnstones, plovers, sandpipers, whimbrels and perhaps storm-petrels on their way between breeding areas and wintering areas around the Indian Ocean. Land birds introduced from Madagascar, Mauritius, Seychelles and India since the nineteenth century include fodies, Madagascar turtle doves, cattle egrets, barred ground doves, mynahs and the domestic fowl which now run wild. Many of the birds of Diego Garcia are beautifully portrayed on the 1990 definitive set of British Indian Ocean Territory postage stamps.

There are no indigenous mammals in Diego Garcia and no sign that any ever existed. Of those introduced in the plantation era, which included horses, cattle, sheep, pigs and dogs, only donkeys, cats and rats have survived and thrived. The wild donkeys could perhaps in due course evolve into a distinctive breed, the Diego donkey. An imaginative proposal to introduce the endangered Rodrigues fruit bat to the island has, for the moment at least, been abandoned.

If Diego Garcia has a native 'king' species it should surely be the giant coconut or robber crabs. Their Creole name is *cipaye* or *sipaille*. The coconut crab has a mottled purplish appearance and can grow to 3 feet across. Their enormous pincers can rip open a coconut husk. They are nocturnal creatures but can be found in the day skulking in holes in the ground or under fallen vegetation. They should be treated with great respect – a writer in 1802 noted that their pincers could snap off the iron tips of walking sticks – but if approached from the right direction (the rear), can be picked up. This, however, requires strong nerve. Other crabs,

the land crab and the fiddler crab, energetically excavate
sandy areas, including in the barochois. On the beach, most
shells on examination are found to be occupied by hermit
crabs and immature coconut crabs.

There are a couple of types of lizard or, more accurately,
geckos on the island, at least one species of toad, but no
snakes. Despite the presence of African bees, hornets, several
variety of spider and one of scorpion, the main hazard when
walking or jogging in the jungle of Diego Garcia is not creepy-
crawlies but being hit on the head by a falling coconut.
Five per cent of the identified insect specimens, including a
butterfly, are unique to the island and there are doubtless
more still to be discovered.

If land fauna on Diego Garcia is admittedly fairly limited,
marine life is exceptionally rich. As Gilbert Bourne wrote in
1886, 'to describe the immense and varied marine fauna
that abounds around this island requires a paper on natural
history'.[3] Spectacular visitors to the shore are two varieties of
large marine turtle, the green and the hawksbill. Their life
span is 150 years and they only start breeding when they are
50. After mating at sea the females come ashore on the high
tide in different seasons according to species, the hawksbill
during the north-west monsoon and the green during the
south-east trades, and lay their numerous eggs, which look
like table-tennis balls, in the sand. The turtles were formerly
hunted for their flesh and their shells by the islanders but
they are now protected by law and it seems likely that these
endangered species are increasing in numbers around the
Chagos. Appropriately, the green and hawksbill turtles are
supporters on the BIOT coat of arms. Smaller species of
turtle live permanently in the lagoon, especially at the southern end.

The deep ocean beyond the reef supports dozens of species
of fish. There are 14 types of shark alone, including the
white, grey, tiger, hammerhead, white tip, black tip, nurse
and sand shark. Tuna, especially the big eye, yellowfin and
skipjack varieties are present in huge quantities. Prized game
fish such as the wahoo, marlin, swordfish, kingfish, sunfish,

mahi mahi, bonito, dorado and barracuda are commonly found. The BIOT administration took steps in 1991 to conserve fish stocks in what is probably the least exploited area of the Indian Ocean by introducing a licensing regime in a 200 mile zone around the Chagos. Sperm whales, which breed to the west of the islands, and dolphins receive specific protection.

Richest of all from an ecological point of view is the reef, which teems with a vast variety of life. The living coral itself is Diego Garcia's chief natural glory and indeed the cause of its very existence. The Chagos Archipelago constitutes one of the great reef systems of the world and probably the most pristine. About 100 species of coral, some very rare, have been identified around Diego Garcia and in its lagoon.

The coral animal itself is a primitive organism known as a polyp. It is akin to a sea anemone and the calcium it extracts from sea-water gradually builds up into a variety of remarkable shapes and sizes. The evocative names given to the differing structures formed give a good idea of their appearance: staghorn, organ-pipe, brain, table, mushroom, moss and so on. The shape of coral rock formed is influenced by the depth at which it grows. The range of colours – yellow, green, pink, blue, violet, brown and grey – is derived from the minute plants which live inside the polyps.

Reef-building corals are delicate and choosy organisms. They are found in a belt around the world in the Indian Ocean, the Pacific and the Caribbean 30 degrees either side of the Equator where the sea temperature is below 100°F (37°C) and above 68°F (20°C). Corals need the right amount of oxygen and salinity in the water. They cannot grow above water and because they need light will not grow much below 150 feet in depth. They like water that is somewhat disturbed but not rough. Consequently, the reef corals are less luxuriant on the south-east side of Diego Garcia which is most exposed to storms.

There are living coral reefs both around and inside the lagoon of Diego Garcia. These are alive with literally hundreds of varieties of small, brilliantly coloured tropical fish such as are found in aquariums all over the world, as well as the larger grouper, snapper, jack, emperor, trevally, moray eel, sting ray and manta ray. Seaweeds in a multiplicity of forms, sea cucumbers, octopuses, crabs, lobsters and small turtles add to the variety. Underwater swimming is a constant delight in Diego Garcia, although in addition to watching out for sharks an eye must be kept open for the sinister stone fish and the scorpion fish with their poisonous spines.

III

From out the Azure Main

Diego Garcia and its sibling islands comprise all that remains above sea-level of huge underwater mountains of volcanic origin which rear dramatically from the ocean bed 10,000 feet or more below. The romantic appellation for these islands is the 'Peaks of Limuria'.

Limuria is the name given to the ancient continent which used to exist in the middle of the Indian Ocean, a sort of Indian Ocean Atlantis. This lost continent was probably created as a result of apocalyptic volcanic activity 130 million years ago as the land mass of what is now India gradually drifted away from Africa. Even now seismic activity is common in the area. A severe earthquake is reported to have occurred in Diego Garcia in 1812 and there was another major one elsewhere in the Chagos Archipelago in 1913. An earthquake measuring as high as 7.6 on the Richter Scale struck Diego Garcia in November 1983. Although causing limited damage to buildings, it ruptured some of the underground fuel lines. Earthquakes of 6.0 or above on the Scale occur regularly. There have been a dozen such occurrences since 1940. Luckily the lack of a wide surrounding platform of shallows precludes the building of tidal waves as a result of seismic activity.

It seems likely that over the aeons of time the sea level in the Indian Ocean waxed and waned as a result both of uplift and subsidence, and of the periodic ice ages which locked up water in the icecaps. Because of the sea level changes during this period, the underlying peaks of basalt became overlaid with coral limestone to a depth of as much as a mile. Only 17,000 years ago, at the end of the last ice age, the sea level was 300 feet lower than at present. This would have meant that, where there are now only banks and atolls, a vastly larger area of dry land would have existed, including the whole of the present Chagos Bank and large adjacent islands.

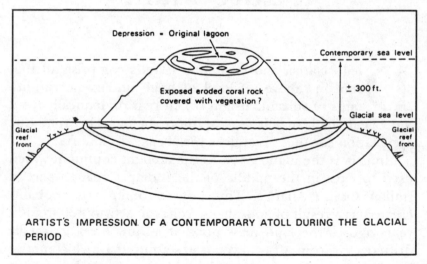

Depression ■ Original lagoon

Contemporary sea level

Exposed eroded coral rock covered with vegetation ?

± 300 ft.

Glacial sea level

Glacial reef front

Glacial reef front

ARTIST'S IMPRESSION OF A CONTEMPORARY ATOLL DURING THE GLACIAL PERIOD

(From book Half of Paradise by Professor David Bellamy)

We cannot know what type of vegetation flourished then or what sort of wildlife roamed the land because, as the Polar icecaps melted, the sea swept in like Noah's flood. The land may well have been entirely submerged. As Lord Tennyson wrote as he came to grips with dawning scientific reality in his poem *In Memoriam,*

There rolls the deep where grew the tree,
Oh earth what changes hast thou seen![1]

Certainly no trace of pre-Holocene, that is before the last ice age, flora and fauna remains, in contrast to the larger land masses in the Western Indian Ocean now comprising Madagascar, Mauritius, Reunion and Seychelles, which had sufficient elevation to avoid being totally engulfed. In these places weird and unique forms of life such as the lemur and, until hunted to extinction, the dodo survived. In fact, the limited range of land flora and fauna in the islands of the Chagos Archipelago suggests that in their latest form they emerged from the sea perhaps only a couple of thousand years ago. Like Britain in the song 'Rule Britannia', Diego Garcia literally 'at heaven's command arose from out the azure main'. Given no further significant changes in sea level during this period and the lack of evidence of major movements of the earth's crust in the area, how could this happen?

The solution to the mystery was first put forward by no less an authority than Charles Darwin, the great nineteenth century natural scientist and author of *The Origin of the Species* which fundamentally altered man's view of the world. In 1842 Darwin published a work called *The Structure and Distribution of Coral Reefs*, which was based on the observations he carried out during his epic four-and-a-half year voyage around the globe on HMS *Beagle*. One of the *Beagle*'s missions was to take soundings around coral islands and to determine if the atolls sat on the summits of extinct volcanoes. Darwin and the *Beagle* visited the Cocos-Keeling Islands and Mauritius in the Indian Ocean but, impatient to return home after such a long voyage, did not call at the Chagos group. However, Darwin drew extensively in his book on coral reefs on a thorough scientific survey of the Chagos, and Diego Garcia in particular, carried out in 1837 by Captain Robert Moresby. As he acknowledged in the preface:

> I must most particularly express my obligations to Captain Moresby, Indian Navy, who conducted the survey of the archipelagos of low coral islands in the Indian Ocean.

According to Darwin's theory, as the sea level rises, the living coral grows up too, keeping pace with and just below the surface of the water. On to this submerged platform wash boulders of dead coral and sand, forming a bank which builds up above high water. Once a dry bank is established it begins to be colonised by seeds of plants and trees borne on the ocean currents. The predominant current washing the Chagos Archipelago is the Malabar current coming from the direction of South-East Asia. It is therefore not surprising that most of the indigenous flora on the islands is of Asian origin. Of these, the key to stabilising the newly emergent islands will have been *Scaevola tacada*, commonly known as 'scavvy' in Diego Garcia, which thrives in sand and does not mind some contact with salt water. It forms a strong and impenetrable thicket along shorelines just above high water. Because of their buoyant water-borne husks the coco-nut and the rose tree will have been among early trees to establish themselves. Ironwoods and the creeper *Caesalpina bonduc* may have arrived as sea-borne seeds floating on vegetal debris. Birds, which can migrate huge distances across the ocean, will also have been the agents of colonisation by bring-ing seeds on their bodies. And their droppings, forming guano, will have helped enrich the poor mixture of sand and coral and thus encouraged further growth of vegetation, which in decay also fertilised the ground.

As Darwin recognised, Diego Garcia is unusual as an atoll in that almost the whole reef around the lagoon has been converted into land, 'an unparalleled case, I believe, in an atoll of such large size', he observed.[2] It seems likely that the present island is the result of the merging of a number of smaller islands that established themselves on the reef. The narrowness of the land at various points and the undeveloped nature of the vegetation, especially on the eastern arm of the island north of Minni Minni, suggests that some of the various individual islands which originally existed were joined up only comparatively recently. This could eventually happen between Eclipse Point and West Island. And a new island is forming at the mouth of the lagoon to the west of Middle

Island at the north-western end of Spurs Reef. This islet was given the name Anniversary Island in honour of the 25th anniversary of the establishment of the British Indian Ocean Territory in November 1990. If it survives, it will be interesting to see how quickly it is colonised by 'scavvy' and coconuts.

Darwin's theory of the origin of atolls is still accepted, although he seems to have been misled by some of Moresby's data to conclude that the Chagos was a dying group of coral atolls sitting on top of subsiding submarine mountains. He does not appear to have taken into account the effect of rises and falls in sea level because of periodic ice ages. He later acknowledged Gilbert Bourne's work on the subject and conceded that in the case of Diego Garcia there was no evidence of subsidence.

The fact that a minute marine creature could be responsible for the creation of solid land can still amaze today as much as it did the great scientists who discovered the phenomenon. Darwin wrote:

> Everyone must be struck with astonishment when he first beholds one of those vast rings of coral rock, often many leagues in diameter, here and there surmounted by a low verdant island with dazzling white shores, bathed on the outside by the foaming breakers of the ocean, and on the inside surrounding a calm expanse of water which from reflection is generally of a bright but pale green colour. The naturalist will feel this astonishment more deeply after having examined the soft and almost gelatinous bodies of those apparently insignificant coral polypifers, and when he knows that the solid reef increases only on the outer edge, which day and night is lashed by the breakers of an ocean never at rest.[3]

Bourne echoed the same sentiment on visiting Diego Garcia itself in 1885:

> The most unimaginative person will not fail to be struck with wonder that the vital activity of animals so low on

the scale as coral polyps has been sufficient to raise up this island above the waves and to maintain it there in spite of the increasing wear and tear to which it is subject from the restless waves of the great southern ocean.[4]

IV

Discovery

The Chagos islands may well have been untouched by human footprints from their formation until the dawn of the modern era. It is possible that the Malagasy may have visited the islands as they made their way around the Indian Ocean from present-day Indonesia to their future home in Madagascar in the early days of the Christian era. It has been suggested that it was they who introduced the coconut and that the old Maldivian name for the islands was of Malagasy origin.[1] The Arabs who reached the Laccadive and Maldive islands immediately to the north in the ninth century may have had some inkling of islands to the south. And a remarkable Chinese expedition during the Ming Dynasty commanded by Cheng Ho, the Great Eunuch of the Imperial Palace, would have sailed close to the Chagos in 1413–15. However, if any of these intrepid voyagers did visit the islands, we shall never know for they left no mark or record.

What is certain is that the Portuguese sighted and named the islands in the early sixteenth century. In the course of the fifteenth century, the traditional route through the Eastern Mediterranean, the Red Sea and the Persian Gulf to the Asian sources of luxuries which Europe sought was blocked by the expansion of the war-like Ottoman Turks. Driven by a mixture of crusading zeal and mercantile enterprise, the Portuguese pioneered an alternative sea route around Africa to India and the Spice Islands in the later fifteenth and early sixteenth centuries. Their route lay across the Indian Ocean.

The actual discoverer of the islands was probably Pedro Mascarenhas, after whom the Mascarene group of islands comprising Mauritius, Reunion and Rodrigues is named. It was the custom of the Portuguese explorers to call newly discovered islands after either captains of vessels or saints' days. There were fleets to the Indian Ocean in 1509 and 1512 commanded by Diego Lopes and Garcia de Naronha respectively. It is tempting to assume that some combination of these names was applied to the largest of the islands that they stumbled on in their caravels and *nãos* far out in the Indian Ocean. According to another account, a Spanish navigator actually named Diego Garcia visited the island in 1532.[2] However, the origin of the name can be no more than speculation. Early maps give a variety of other names including Gratia, Graciosa, Don Garzia and Chagos island. The existing name only became definitive towards the end of the eighteenth century. The Portuguese names for other groups in the Archipelago also stuck, Peros Banhos, and Three Brothers, which is a translation of the Portuguese 'Três Irmãos'.

The only evidence found in Diego Garcia of Portuguese visits are the roof tiles brought up by divers from the floor of the lagoon in Rambler Bay. It was the custom to carry such items on the outward voyage from Portugal as ballast which could be put to good use on arrival before loading up with spices, calicoes, muslins and chinaware for the return trip. There may well be Portuguese wrecks in other parts of the Archipelago. One fairly well-documented case is that of a *não* (a type of sailing ship of about 500 tons, named the *Conceição* (*Conception*) which was outward bound from Lisbon to Goa in India with a cargo of jewels, gold and silver in 1555 when it ran aground on the reefs of Peros Banhos.[3] The captain Francisco Nombre and other officers appropriated

HRH the Duke of York on Diego Garcia with the author, November 1988.
(NSF Fotolab, Diego Garcia)

East Point chapel. *(NSF Fotolab, Diego Garcia)*

Manager's house, East Point plantation. *(NSF Fotolab, Diego Garcia)*

Lagoon just before sunset. *(Dan Layman)*

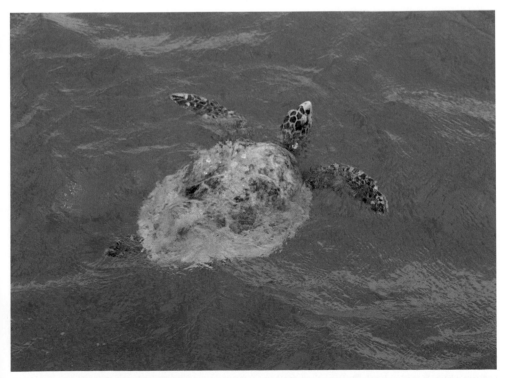

A green turtle in the lagoon.

A coconut crab. *(Dan Layman)*

Reef life. *(USN Diving Locker, Diego Garcia)*

A family of red-footed boobies. *(Dan Layman)*

A takamaka tree. *(John Topp)*

Flower of a rose tree. *(John Topp)*

A sixteenth-century Portuguese map of the Indian Ocean. *(The British Library)*

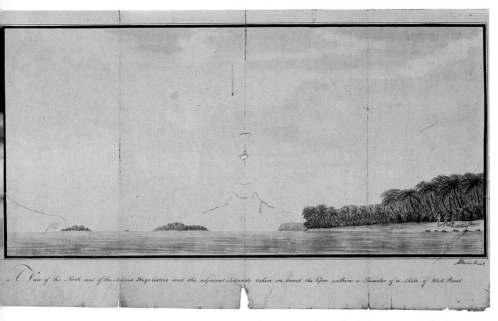

View of the north end of Diego Garcia; 1786; watercolour by Lieutenant Wales.
(India Office Collection, British Library)

The settlement at East Point, 1819; Dutch print by Lieutenant Verhuell.
(Mr K. Dirkzwager)

Six-inch naval guns at Cannon Point, installed in 1942. *(NSF Fotolab, Diego Garcia)*

Wreck of RAF Catalina beached in 1944 at East Point. *(NSF Fotolab, Diego Garcia)*

the only undamaged boat, filled it with as much treasure as it could carry and set out for India, leaving 350 crew and passengers to fend for themselves. Of these 50 eventually managed to reach India in improvised craft but the rest perished from hunger and exposure. It is possible that remains of the *Conceição*'s equipment and cargo could still be found.

Among the rare references to the Chagos in this period is the claim to them made by the Christian King of the Maldives, Dom Manuel, who was installed by the Portuguese in the mid-sixteenth century. The islands were called 'Folovahi' in the Maldivian language Divehi, which means something like 'ten islands'. However, two attempts by the Maldivians to colonise the islands failed when they could not locate them.

The discovery of the Chagos Archipelago was a minor incidental by-product of the opening up of the seaway from Europe to the Indies. The islands were not on the main route, which followed the African coast to around the latitude of present-day Kenya and then struck out towards India. Accordingly they were not regarded as of any value as way-stations for water and fresh supplies. On the contrary, the Chagos Archipelago with its network of dangerous reefs was seen as a peril to be given a wide berth. The inaccuracy of the charts, which scattered islands, many of them imaginary, over a wide area increased the uncertainty of navigation in the central Indian Ocean.

The English, along with the French and Dutch, began to follow the route pioneered by the Portuguese to the lucrative *entrepôts* of the East in the later sixteenth century. The experience of the captain of one of the first English fleets to penetrate the Indian Ocean graphically illustrates the perils posed to early navigators in the seas around the Chagos. Setting out from Agalega Island north-east of Madagascar in the direction of India in late March 1602 Sir James Lancaster found himself two weeks later trapped within the reefs of the Chagos Bank. For several days the ships tried to find a way out of the maze or 'pound' (enclosure) as Lancaster called it. Eventually, led by a small boat from which constant sounding of the depth was made, the fleet was able, 'thanks be to God', to nose gingerly out of the reefs to the open ocean to the north and continue its voyage.

Although Lancaster did not land on any of the islands in the Chagos he left a vivid account of his earlier landfall at Agalega, an island which shares many of the same characteristics:

> As we coasted along this island, it seemed very fair and pleasant, exceeding full of fowl [birds] and coconut trees; and there came from the land such a pleasant smell as if it had been a garden of flowers.[4]

For a further century and a half, after Lancaster's inadvertent visit, although the Dutch established themselves from 1639 in Mauritius and the French from 1654 in Reunion, the Chagos remained in a sort of limbo, vaguely in the consciousness but rarely visited by the European nations contending for the upper hand in the Indian Ocean. If pirates, who in the early eighteenth century established a shortlived stronghold in eastern Madagascar and bases in the Seychelles, ever used or visited Diego Garcia, there is no record of this but the intriguing possibility cannot be discounted. An eighteenth century cannon-ball was discovered in the jungle on the eastern arm of the island in 1989. And a mid-nineteenth century ordinance reserved to the Crown any buried treasure found on Diego Garcia.

As time went on, the contest in the Indian Ocean became increasingly one between Britain and France, with India as the prize. The five wars fought by the two countries in the course of the eighteenth century spilled over into eastern seas. Meanwhile the French were assiduously island-hopping. In 1722 they took over Mauritius which the Dutch had abandoned in 1703, and renamed it the Ile de France. They also colonised Rodrigues 300 miles to the east in 1742.

From the 1740s the French began systematically to survey the islands to the north and the north-east of their principal base on Mauritius. Up to this point these islands remained inaccurately fixed, still unknown, or even figments of the imagination, as was the case in their rendering in the chart the 'English Pilot' published in 1755. The co-ordinator of this effort was the renowned French cartographer Après de Mannevillette who embodied his findings in his famous map of the Indian Ocean 'Neptune Oriental', published in 1780. Much of this effort of filling in the gaps on the map was directed towards the north where Mahé in the Seychelles group was first formally possessed in 1756 and then colonised in 1768. However, several expeditions visited the Chagos. In 1770 a Monsieur la Fontaine in the vessel *L'Heure du Berger* surveyed the northern part of the lagoon at Diego Garcia and produced the first detailed map of the island. This ship also achieved the feat of sailing the dangerous passage between East Island and Barton Point. Subsequently a British ship, the *Hampshire*, was wrecked attempting the passage in 1793. Elsewhere in the Archipelago, in 1777, the French ship *Salomon* visited and named the islands of that name in the northern Chagos.

The British, from their bases in India, were also showing an interest in the islands. In 1760 the *Egmont* visited the islands which bear its name. In 1763 the *Speaker* and the *Pitt* surveyed the banks named after them and also visited Diego Garcia, producing a rough sketch from the north which may be the first known pictorial rendering of the island. In 1772 the *Eagle* called at the island of the same name. And in 1774 the *Drake* visited Diego Garcia and carried out a detailed survey of the entrance to the lagoon, including detailed sketches by a Joseph Mascall which show West, Middle and East islands, which were named respectively Red Beach, Black Beach and White Beach islands on the picture. This expedition left sheep, goats and pigs on the island as fresh provisions for future expeditions.

On the British side, the driving force in mapping the islands of the Central Indian Ocean was Scotsman Alexander Dalrymple, the Hydrographer of the East Indian Company, who published in 1786 a *Memoir concerning the Chagos Archipelago and the Adjacent Islands*. Dalrymple sent orders from

London to the Company's base in Bombay to despatch vessels:

> to ascertain the numerous shoals and islands in the Southern Passage from the Maldives to Madagascar as an accurate knowledge of these hitherto much neglected Seas is essential to the security of the Navigation of the Company's ships.[5]

As a result of these instructions, a comprehensive exploration of the Archipelago was undertaken by Lieutenant Archibald Blair of the East India Company Marine in 1786 and 1787. He was given orders that:

> for facilitating the more particular survey of the island afterwards, he was to leave a distinguishing mark on all the principal points, which should terminate his angles, or form stations, to enable those points to be found at any future time.[6]

Accordingly, in May 1786, Blair carried out a survey of Diego Garcia, setting up flag staffs at key places to act as reference points. Although he was given only a couple of weeks for the undertaking, Blair produced a highly accurate map which would pass muster today. He also observed the eclipse of Jupiter's moons, which no doubt accounts for the names Eclipse and Observatory Points at the entrance to the Diego Garcia lagoon.

The transformation in knowledge about the Chagos resulting from these systematic surveys meant that, in future, mariners would avoid the experience of James Horsburgh, who later succeeded Dalrymple as the East India Company Hydrographer. In May 1786 he was wrecked on Diego Garcia in the *Atlas* on the point on the east coast which bears his name:

> The charts on board were very erroneous in their rendering of the Chagos Islands and Banks and the Com-

mander trusting too much to dead reckoning was steering with confidence to make Ady or Candy (islands which turned out not to exist) . . . but unfortunately, a cloud over Diego Garcia prevented the helmsman from discerning it (the officer of the watch being asleep) till we were on the reef close to the shore; the masts, rudder and everything above deck went with the first surge; the second lifted the vessel over the outer rocks and threw her in toward the beach, it being high water and the vessel in ballast, otherwise, she must have been dashed in pieces by two or three surfs on the outer part of the reef and every person on board have perished.[7]

The survivors from the ill-fated *Atlas* were rescued by the expedition described in the next chapter.

V

Settlement

A Monsieur Dupuit de la Faye was given a grant of Diego Garcia by the Governor of Mauritius in 1778 and there is evidence of temporary French sojourns. However, the first systematic attempt to colonise the island was made by the British. In 1786 the East India Company, the great commercial corporation which established and ran Britain's Empire in the East for 250 years, decided that it was now feasible to establish a victualling station where, as Dalrymple put it:

> ships might be enabled to get refreshments after their long voyage from Europe before they came into the low latitudes where the light winds and tedious passages consequent to them, had so often proved fatal to the lives of the seamen before they could reach India.[1]

It was also hoped that Diego Garcia could be a base for further exploration of the islands of the central Indian Ocean, as well as in future wars against France.

The aim was that the new settlement should be self-sufficient. According to the reports available, Diego Garcia had good water, soil which would support 'legumes' (vegetables) and an abundance of fish, turtles and 'land lobsters'. The latter 'fed on coconuts and are very good, their tails very fat'.[2] The expedition was to take with it boatloads of soil and to experiment with the growing of grain, fruit and vegetables. It was also to bring cattle and poultry.

After meticulous planning, the expedition set out from Bombay on 15 March 1786 in four ships, the *Admiral Hughes*, the *Drake* and the survey ships *Viper* and *Experiment*. Richard Price and John Smyth, senior officials of the East India Company, were respectively first and second in command. Price was appointed 'Resident of Diego Garcia', effectively the first British representative. The civilian element included carpenters, smiths, bricklayers, coopers, stockmen, gardeners, bakers, butchers, tailors and two doctors as well as 50 servants. An engineering officer Captain Sartorius commanded the military element, who were all volunteers. This consisted of 64 Indian infantry sepoys and 2 bandsmen, 24 Indian engineer pioneers and a number of marine surveying officers led by Lieutenant Blair, mentioned in Chapter IV. They also took with them one field piece and 6 or 8 pieces of smaller artillery.

The expedition sailed with sealed orders to be opened at sea in order to keep its destination secret from the French. The instructions included contingency plans in case any French were encountered on the island. If 'beyond all expectations ... a regular settlement ... who cannot be removed by force were found, new orders were to be sought. However, if only 'straggling French' were present these were to be 'deemed to be there without authority and not any impediment to occupying the island and establishing a settlement'.[3] In fact when the expedition entered the lagoon of Diego Garcia on 27 April 1786, they were surprised to see a canoe set out from the shore with five men on board who produced papers from a Monsieur Le Normand about his establishment on the island, which consisted of 'a dozen huts of the meanest appearance'. The British expedition chose not to regard this as evidence of a proper French title to the island and on 4 May 'took formal possession of the island of

Diego Garcia and all its Dependencies in the name of His Majesty King George the Third and in the name and for the use of the Honourable United Company'.[4] The hoisting of the British flag was saluted with three volleys of musketry. The East India Company's own flag, on which the American Stars and Stripes was modelled, will also have been flown by the expedition. The Frenchmen found on the island left for Mauritius to report this turn of events.

Meanwhile, the expedition got down to its task of laying out a settlement, building a fort, planting crops, measuring temperatures and winds and surveying the land and the lagoon. A Lieutenant Wales produced charming water-colour sketches of the island, one of which showed three men in broad-brimmed hats and knee-breeches strolling on the shore among the crabs near Cannon Point, and another of two of the expedition's ships sailing across the mouth of the lagoon. The settlement was established on the site of the present East Point, which was named Flag Staff Point. The climate was found to be quite healthy and few men fell sick. Temperatures taken over a four week period between early May and early June showed a range of 73°F to 87°F (approximately 23°C to 31°C), which is remarkably consistent with present-day readings. However, the agricultural experiments were disappointing. Vegetables such as potatoes and grain would grow but the amazing swarms of rats caused problems. Most of the turkeys and ducks died and the cattle sickened. There were also disagreements over whether the island was militarily defensible and who was responsible for surveying the lagoon.

The reports from Price and Smyth to the Council in Bombay sowed doubts about the settlement's viability. The Directors of the East India Company in London also became concerned when they learned of the expedition's 'magnitude and unnecessary cost.'[5] A further problem was that the French were exercised by the establishment of the settlement. The Governor of Mauritius, the Vicomte de Souillac, sent a letter of protest to Bombay. An international incident seemed likely to develop. Accordingly the Bombay Council decided in August 1786 'to entirely withdraw the settlement from

Diego Garcia'. A letter from Bombay Castle signed by Governor Rawson Hart Boddam (after whom Boddam island in the Salomons is named) instructed Price and Smyth that 'on receipt of this letter you will immediately issue the necessary orders for the embarkation of the stores, ammunition and provisions and for evacuating the island'.[6] The expedition sailed away in October 1786, leaving Lieutenant Blair to complete his survey of the rest of the Archipelago.

The French authorities in Mauritius were sufficiently alarmed by news of the British settlement to send the frigate *Minerva* to enforce their claim and eject the interlopers. However, by the time the French ship arrived, the British had already left. The French none the less put up a stone pillar proclaiming their sovereignty. A similar marker decorated with fleur de lys survives at Mahé in the Seychelles but that on Diego Garcia has disappeared; perhaps it still lies somewhere on the island awaiting discovery.

The British incursion led the French to take a more active interest in the islands. In the later 1780s businessmen in Mauritius were granted concessions to gather coconuts. A petition to operate in one of the islands reads 'this desert island uninhabited up to the time of writing, can nevertheless hold out prospects to an industrious and enterprising man.'[7] The first named individual to receive this concession in Diego Garcia was the same Monsieur Le Normand whom the British encountered in 1786. A Sieur Dauguet was also granted fishing rights. It is not clear whether these concessions involved the setting up of permanent establishments or merely limited visits. The French in Mauritius also seem to have begun using Diego Garcia as a leper colony, apparently in the belief that turtle meat helped to cure this condition. According to one account, a British ship anchored off Diego Garcia in 1792 and sent ashore two Lascars or Indian seamen to look for water. These encountered a small party of lepers. When they reported the fact on coming back on board, such was the fear of leprosy in those days that the ship's master put the Lascars ashore to fend for themselves – a nightmare story if true.

In 1793, a Mr Lapotaire of Port Louis proposed to the French authorities that instead of loose coconuts being brought back to Mauritius from Diego Garcia for processing, a 'factory' be established to extract copra and oil from them on the island. Lapotaire sent out two ships with 25 to 30 men in each and a complement of slaves to set up the enterprise, which could be termed Diego Garcia's Jamestown, and seems to have been based at the north-west corner of the island. By the next year, Lapotaire was exporting a considerable amount of oil to Mauritius. According to Baron d'Unienville, salted fish, and rope made of coconut fibre were also exported, and sea slugs to the Far East, where they were a sought-after delicacy among the Chinese.[8]

There was good profit in the extraction of coconut oil which was used for a variety of purposes including lamps, cooking and soap. In the 1790's France was again at war with Britain and Mauritius found itself increasingly cut off from longer distance trade by the British blockade, leading among other things to a steep rise in oil prices. It is therefore not surprising that other businessmen from Mauritius began to follow Lapotaire's example and to set up their own establishments in Diego Garcia, as well as in other islands of the Chagos Archipelago. On Diego Garcia two brothers, Paul and Aimé Cayeux established themselves at East Point and Minni Minni.

While Lapotaire and the Cayeux seem to have had no problems in dividing the island between them, in the early 1800s they united against two newcomers, Messrs Blévec and Chepé, whom they accused of wasteful exploitation of the coconuts. However, in 1809 the French Captain General of Mauritius, De Caen, settled the dispute by assigning eastern parts of the island to Blévec and Chepé, while forbidding the manufacture of oil in Diego Garcia on the grounds that this would attract British raids. Readiness to accept lepers sent from Mauritius was a condition of the concessions.

But French rule in the Indian Ocean was about to be snuffed out at its heart. Exasperated by French privateer attacks on British shipping, a British expeditionary force from

India captured Rodrigues and Reunion and finally Mauritius itself. The capitulation signed on 3 December 1810 marked 'the surrender of the Isle of France (Mauritius) and all its dependencies (including the Chagos) to the arms of His Britannic Majesty'. The Treaty of Paris signed in May 1814 formally ceded 'the Isle of France and all its dependencies ... to the dominions of the British Crown'. The Chagos Archipelago has remained British territory ever since.

Although the formal period of French rule on Diego Garcia was quite short, by the time it ended the pattern of a plantation society based on exploitation of the coconut, which was to last more than another century and a half, was well established. A contemporary Dutch print of East Point dating from 1819 is the first known depiction of the settlement.[9] It was probably made by a naval officer called Verhuell who was a survivor of the crew of the Dutch warship *Admiral Evertsen*, which was carrying home from Java spices, some 'boxes with curiosities' for the King of the Netherlands, senior officials of the Dutch East India Company and an admiral. The ship foundered off Diego Garcia on 9 April 1819 and the 340-strong crew were rescued by the American brig *Pickering*, a vessel of 154 tons from Plymouth, Massachusetts,[10] which is shown at anchor in the print. Two hundred of the rescued sailors spent many weeks on the island before another ship arrived to take them off.

The Dutch print shows manually driven copra mills, simple buildings and huts, loin-clothed slaves carrying between them a turtle, fish and baskets, and overdressed Europeans promenading with walking sticks. Dogs (one appears in the print), cats, pigs, poultry, bees, new plants and vegetables would have been introduced by this point. Rats had also been inadvertently introduced from visiting ships at an early stage and soon became a menace to bird life, which had not previously experienced predators.

The population in 1826 was 275, made up of 6 Europeans, only one of whom was female; 14 freemen, four of whom were female, and 9 were children; 218 slaves, of whom 17 were female and 13 children; and 37 lepers, 5 of whom were female and 2 were children.[11] Most of the slaves would have been brought from Mozambique and Madagascar either directly or through Mauritius and Seychelles. As a *lingua franca* they would soon have adopted Creole, a dialect of French with African overtones, whose use was universal in France's tropical possessions and is still spoken by Mauritians working in Diego Garcia today.

In the tiny society of the islands and far from assistance in Mauritius, it does not seem from contemporary accounts that the overseers actively mistreated the slaves. The historian Charles Pridham, who visited the island soon after the abolition of slavery, noted that their set tasks involving the collection and preparation of coconuts were relatively light and their rations of rice and rum could be supplemented by what they could catch or raise for themselves. According to d'Unienville, the latter included fish caught at night by torchlight, birds knocked from their perches by long sticks, *cipaye* crabs, and of course coconuts. As elsewhere in slave societies the considerable imbalance between the sexes and the lack of a religious or moral framework gave rise to considerable promiscuity. Their overseers seem to have provided little better example. As Pridham priggishly remarked, 'Frenchmen when removed from the public eye, have a strong tendency to degenerate into savages'.[12]

VI

Abolition of Slavery

Especially in an age of *laissez-faire* or self-regulation, the new British administration in Mauritius might have been content to leave the planters to their own devices in far off Diego Garcia had it not been for the issue of slavery. The slave trade in the British Empire had been abolished in 1807. Sir Robert Farquhar, the first British Governor of Mauritius and its dependencies, made it clear to the new subjects of the Crown in a proclamation of 1815 that 'no doubt should exist that Acts of Parliament for the abolition of the Trade in Slaves extend to every, *even the most remote and minute portion*, of the Possession, Dominions and Dependencies of His Majesty's Government'.[1] Complete abolition of slavery was already in the wind because of pressure from public opinion in Britain.

Nevertheless, despite the attentions of the Royal Navy, slaving to the islands directly from the East African coast probably persisted surreptitiously for some years. At the time of emancipation in the mid-1830s, there were still 33 slaves in Diego Garcia declared as having been born in either Mozambique or Madagascar.

It was unrest on the island because of problems between the planters, the slaves and the lepers (who were still being sent there) which led to the appointment of the first British official, a Mr Le Camus, in Diego Garcia in 1824. Le Camus was also charged with managing the anchorage at Diego Garcia and establishing a quarantine station for seafarers with infectious diseases on one of the islands at the mouth of the lagoon. For his services over a five-year period, Le Camus was granted the concession formerly held by Lapotaire, from whom he bought slaves, stock and buildings.

As in the rest of the British Empire the institution of slavery was formally abolished in Mauritius and its dependencies in August 1834. For a six-year transitional period, so that both masters and slaves could get used to the new situation, the ex-slaves were apprenticed to their former masters under various safeguards. The Act of Parliament ending slavery laid down that Governors of Colonies should appoint Special Commissioners with the powers of Justices of the Peace to implement its provisions. The remoteness of the Indian Ocean dependencies posed special difficulties for the emancipation process but the authorities in Mauritius showed great conscientiousness. A report to the Colonial Office in London in 1835 assured the latter that 'all that can be done to carry into effect the provisions of the Abolition Act as far as circumstances will possibly admit'[2] was being done.

Mr George Harrison, designated as Assistant Protector of Slaves, visited the Chagos islands, including Diego Garcia, to supervise emancipation of the former slaves in 1835. There was a follow-up visit by Special Justice Charles Anderson in 1838 in the brig HMS *Leveret*. His instructions before departure pointed out that as the islands could be visited only occasionally, and his stay would be limited, his object was:

> to acquire information with a view to ulterior improvement if required rather than temporary exercise of authority. You will explain to apprentices in the presence of their masters and overseers their positions under the Slavery Abolition Act . . . the work they are expected to do . . . the treatment they have a right to expect . . . and the nature and quantity of their provisions.[3]

Anderson was also to report on general matters and on the possible value of Diego Garcia as a convict settlement.

Anderson was obviously a zealous person. He not only produced a highly critical report of conditions in Diego Garcia, which he described as 'decidedly inferior to those of labourers on the other islands I have visited',[4] but also exceeded his instructions by intervening actively and ordering the reduction of the daily set tasks of the labourers which he regarded as too severe. He found that the food, consisting mainly of rice, and the clothing provided were unsatisfactory. He described the physical state of the labourers as deplorable, with many of them old, infirm or diseased, with several bad cases of leprosy. There was also a deplorable – a word Anderson obviously liked – deficiency of hospital accommodation and an entire want of medical aid.

On the positive side, Anderson found that the labour involved in coconut plantations was of a much milder nature than on the sugar plantations of Mauritius. Crime was also uncommon, which he attributed to the absence of strong liquor.

Anderson recommended that the proprietors of the plantations resident in Mauritius, who still included Monsieur Cayeux, 'ought to be compelled to make good the past deficiencies to their fullest extent and that other means should be adopted to prevent the repetition of such wilful neglect'.[5] However, the Governor decided more judiciously that while he 'cannot but regret that the Act is not fully complied with . . . yet taking into consideration the locality, the precarious nature and infrequency of communications, he did not feel disposed to visit on the masters the whole penalties for breaches of the law.'[6]

At the time of Anderson's visit there were 135 apprentices, that is, freed slaves, on Diego Garcia. The three estates at East Point, Point Marianne and Minni Minni produced between them 36,000 veltes (a velte is about $3/4$ gallons or nearly 8 litres) of coconut oil annually. Anderson also noted that the island was much resorted to by whalers and vessels bound from England to India for supplies of water, firewood, pork and poultry.

The main difference after final emancipation in 1840, was that the now free labourers made a contract with their new employers in return for wages. Apart from this, life on the islands continued much as before. As Pridham remarked in 1845, 'the slaves on the Chagos Group are now free, that is to say nominally, though perhaps very little change would be found in their condition'.[7] Unlike in Mauritius, where the abolition of slavery led to the increasing recruitment of indentured labour from India to work the sugar plantations, the workers in the islands had effectively nowhere else to go and no other occupation to turn to.

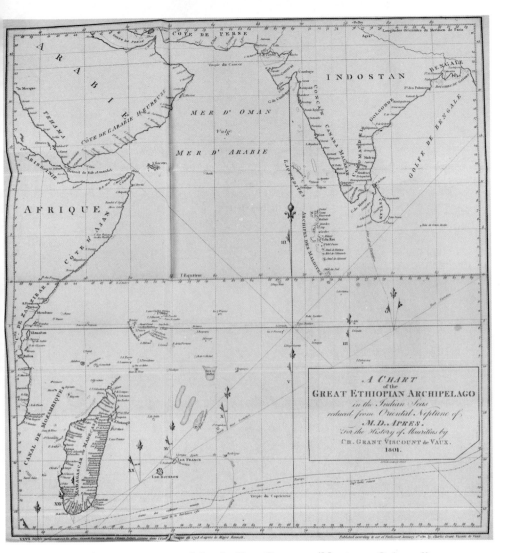

Late eighteenth-century map of the Indian Ocean – 'Neptune Oriental'
– by Apres de Mannevillette. *(India Office Collection, British Library)*

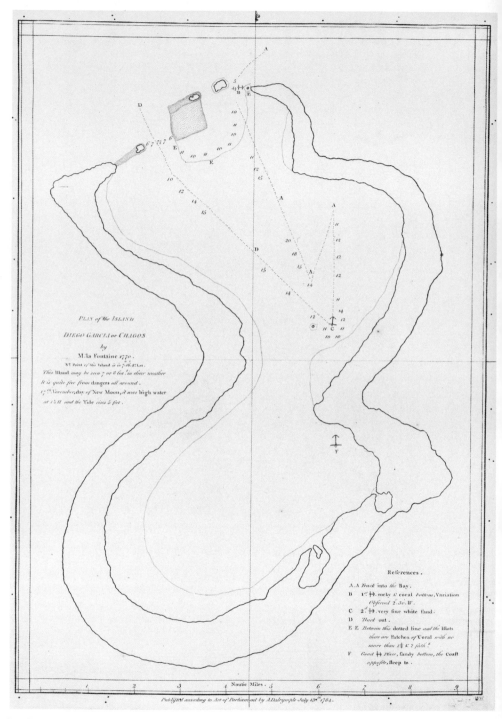

La Fontaine's map of Diego Garcia, published in 1784.
(India Office Collection, British Library)

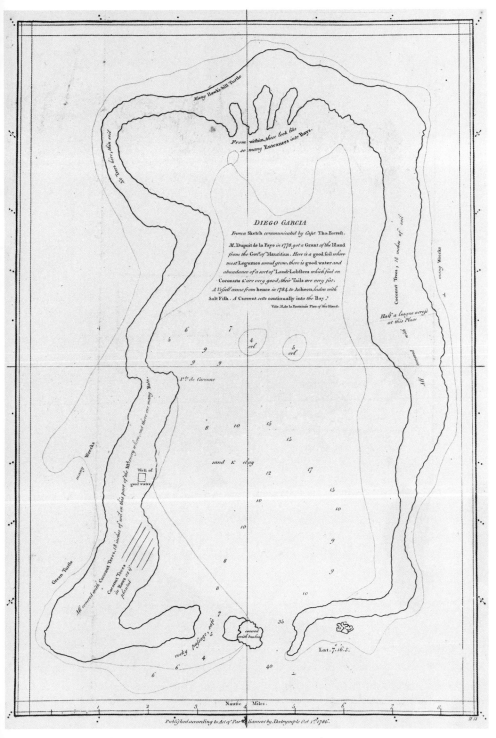

DIEGO GARCIA

From a Sketch communicated by Capt. Tho. Forrest.

*M. Dupuit de la Faye in 1778, got a Grant of the Island
from the Gov.r of Mauritius. Here is a good soil where
most Legumes sowed grow, there is good water and
abundance of a sort of Land-Lobsters which feed on
Coconuts & are very good, their Tails are very fat.
A Vessell came from hence in 1784 to Acheen, laden with
Salt Fish. A Current setts continually into the Bay?*

Vide M.de la Fontaine's Plan of this Island.

Many Hawks-bill Turtle

*From within, these look like
so many Entrances into Bays.*

N.o Trees here thin soil

Coconut Trees, 18 inches of soil

many Wrecks

Half a league across
at this Place

P.te de Caracne

6   7
5   4
crl   5
9   crl
9   9

8   10   15
15
sand & clay   12   17
15
Well of
good water   10   10
10
All covered with Coconut Trees, 18 inches of soil on this part of the Isl. every where, and there are many Rats
Coconut Trees
in Rows or if
planted
many Wrecks
8   9
8
9
10
Green Turtle
7
rocky passage, soft
6   4
covered
with bushes
35
Lat. 7. 16. 5.
6
40

Nautic   Miles.

Published according to Act of Parliament by Dalrymple Oct.r 1.st 1786.

Captain Forrest's map of Diego Garcia, published in 1786.
(India Office Collection, British Library)

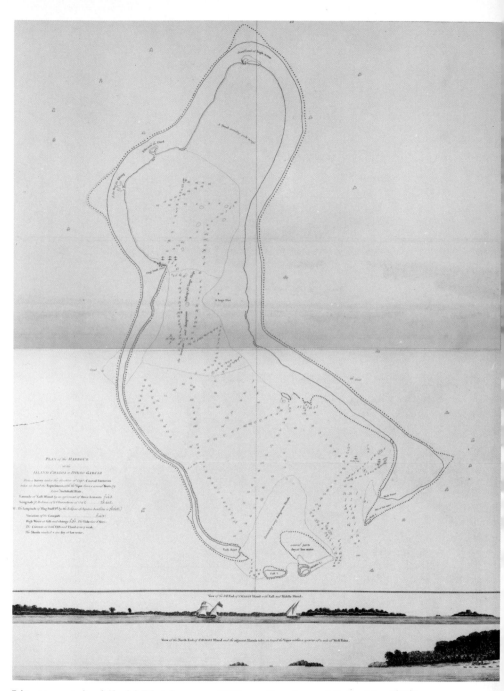

Lieutenant Archibald Blair's map of Diego Garcia, published in 1787.
(India Office Collection, British Library)

The German cruiser SMS *Emden*. *(MOD Library)*

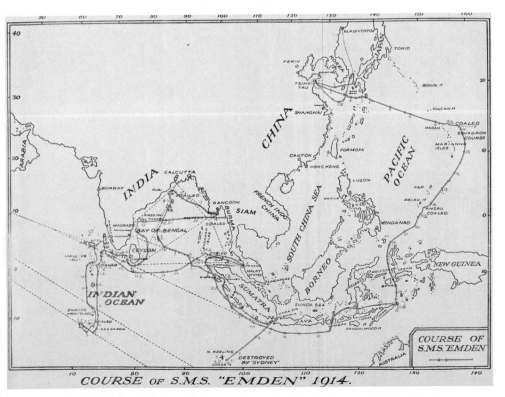

Course of SMS *Emden* 1914. *(From* My Experiences in SMS Emden *by F.J. Hohenzollern)*

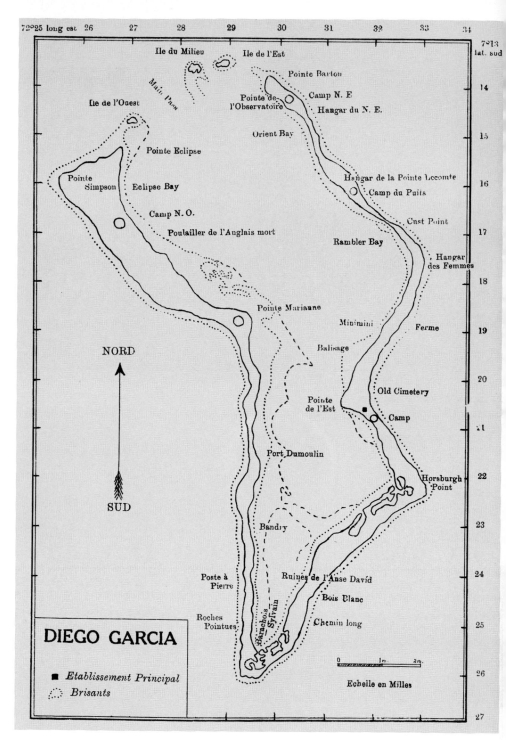

Dussercle's map of Diego Garcia in 1934.
(From Archipel de Chagos: en mission *by R. Dussercle)*

Father Dussercle (seated left with beard) with British military party on Diego Garcia, 1942. *(Fred Barnett – seated next to Dussercle with dog)*

Military burial on Diego Garcia, 1942. Sgt. Fred Barnett marked on photograph with a cross. *(Fred Barnett)*

General view of the Downtown area. *(NSF Fotolab, Diego Garcia)*

BIOT Customs and Immigration officers at the airport. *(NSF Fotolab, Diego Garcia)*

Two flags outside the headquarters building. *(NSF Fotolab, Diego Garcia)*

HRH Prince Edward (in hat) with Commissioner Harris (left) Inspecting old oil grinder at East Point, October 1992. *(NSF Fotolab, Diego Garcia)*

VII

The Oil Island

After emancipation had been implemented, direct British intervention in the affairs of the islands was limited for another quarter of a century. Subject to occasional inspections by captains of visiting Royal Navy ships and Special Commissioners, the islands were run effectively as private estates. The owners of the concessions, or *jouissances* in French, which was still the language in general use, were invariably absentees based in Mauritius.

Two significant developments during this period were the change in the system of tenure and the amalgamation of the plantations. From 1865 the holders of the concessions were able to transform them into permanent holdings against payment based on estimates of the amount of oil produced. In 1883 the three separate existing plantations on Diego Garcia at East Point, Minni Minni and Point Marianne were merged into the 'Société Huilière de Diégo et Péros' (the Diego and Peros Oil Company), which continued to run them, along with those in the outer islands, until 1962.

The running of the plantation was in the hands of an *administrateur*, or manager, assisted by a number of under-managers. These were normally whites from Mauritius. Much of the supervision of the labourers recruited from Mauritius,

Madagascar and Mozambique was left to black *commandeurs* or overseers. Occasionally there was an administrator who by his personality and energy stood out from the run of the mill. One such was James Spurs who ran East Point Plantation as a benevolent despot in the 1870s, among other things showing concern for conservation by forbidding the killing of seabirds, turtles and land crabs.

By the lights of the time, and it should be remembered that slavery persisted in the USA until 1864 and in Brazil until 1888, the management seems to have been reasonably enlightened and humane and the life of the labourers tolerable. Typical wages were 40 dollars a month for an under-manager, 10–14 dollars for an overseer, 5 dollars for crafts-men such as blacksmiths, 4 dollars for field-hands and 3 dollars for the women who shelled the coconuts. The workers were expected to put in a couple of hours of voluntary work on Sunday mornings, known as the *corvée*, to clean up the settlement area and tend the animals.

Huts in the 'camp' for accommodation, and basic rations, were provided. Rations consisted typically of $12^1/_2$ lbs of rice a week, 1lb of salt a month, and 'as gratification' a glass of rum or 'calou' a day 'drunk at the tub as in Her Majesty's Navy.'[1] and an ounce of tobacco a week. Women with babies were entitled to a bottle of coconut oil a week. The labourers supplemented these rations by raising pigs and chickens and by cultivating fruit and vegetables in gardens enclosed to protect them from the depredations of donkeys and crabs. Fish also varied the diet. Such was the abundance of fish that it was said by a visiting official that 'the inhabitants can literally walk into the water and in a few minutes get a supply as would be a banquet for many of a far superior class in Mauritius'.[2]

There were company shops at each of the plantations, selling basic items such as kettles, pans, hooks and needles and small luxuries such as wine, coffee and eau-de-cologne. There was free, if basic, medical care provided for the treatment of the sick and injured. A stock of medicines was dispensed by a medical attendant whose qualifications seem to

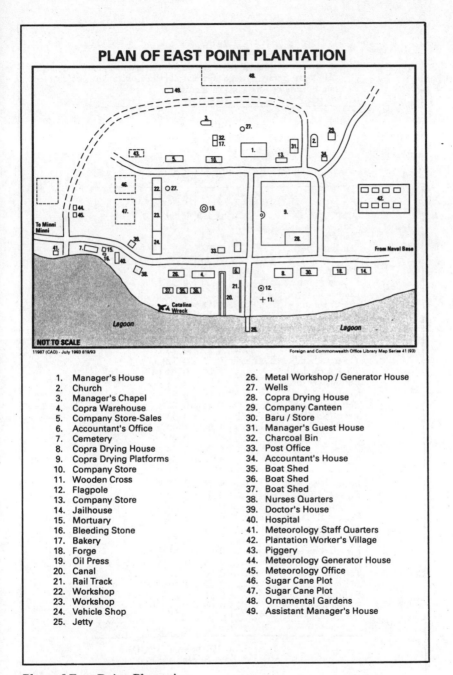

PLAN OF EAST POINT PLANTATION

NOT TO SCALE

11987 (CAD) - July 1993 819/93

Foreign and Commonwealth Office Library Map Series 41 (93)

1. Manager's House
2. Church
3. Manager's Chapel
4. Copra Warehouse
5. Company Store-Sales
6. Accountant's Office
7. Cemetery
8. Copra Drying House
9. Copra Drying Platforms
10. Company Store
11. Wooden Cross
12. Flagpole
13. Company Store
14. Jailhouse
15. Mortuary
16. Bleeding Stone
17. Bakery
18. Forge
19. Oil Press
20. Canal
21. Rail Track
22. Workshop
23. Workshop
24. Vehicle Shop
25. Jetty
26. Metal Workshop / Generator House
27. Wells
28. Copra Drying House
29. Company Canteen
30. Baru / Store
31. Manager's Guest House
32. Charcoal Bin
33. Post Office
34. Accountant's House
35. Boat Shed
36. Boat Shed
37. Boat Shed
38. Nurses Quarters
39. Doctor's House
40. Hospital
41. Meteorology Staff Quarters
42. Plantation Worker's Village
43. Piggery
44. Meteorology Generator House
45. Meteorology Office
46. Sugar Cane Plot
47. Sugar Cane Plot
48. Ornamental Gardens
49. Assistant Manager's House

Plan of East Point Plantation
(Charles Borman and Foreign and Commonwealth Office Library)

Appendix No. 9.

List of Prices at which Articles are supplied to Laborers on Minimini- Estate, Diego Garcia, together with the retail prices of the same in Mauritius.

Articles.	Price on Minimini Estate.	Price in Mauritius.	Remaks.
	$ ₡	$ ₡	
Sugar per lb.	0 12½	0 09	
Coffe do.	0 40	0 30	
Biscuits do.	0 15	0 15	
Salt Pork do.	0 03	...	Made on the Island.
Soap per bar of 2¼ lbs	0 25	..	Do. do.
Wine per bottle	0 25	0 12½	
Liqueurs do.	0 50	0 25	
Conjon bleu per piece	4 00	2 00	
Coutil per aune	0 25	0 18	
Paliacats each	0 37½	0 15	
Grey Calico per piece	4 00	2 25	
White Calico do.	4 00	2 50	24 yards.
Patna each	1 12½	0 75	
Cooured handkerchiefs each	0 25	0 12½	
Thread per bobbin	0 04	0 04	100 yards.
Buttons per dozen	0 12½	0 04	
Needles do.	0 06	0 03	
Thimbles each	0 12½	0 03	
Straw hats (Seychelles) each	1 00	0 50	
Felt hats each	1 50	1 00	
Spoons do.	0 06	0 03	
Forks do.	0 06	0 03	
Plates do.	0 12½	0 06	
Common round dishes each	0 40	0 25	
Basins large each	0 25	0 15	
Knives (sailor's) each	0 25	0 12½	
Marmittes each	0 37½	0 25	
Pagne (Madagascar) each...	0 20	0 12½	
Tobacco per stick each	0 12½	0 08	
Vermouth per bottle.	1 00	0 50	
Fish Hooks large each	0 03	0 01½	
Do. small do.	0 -02	0 00½	
Tin pots each	0 50	0 12½	
Tin mugs each ,.....	0 25	0 12½	
Padlocks	0 50	0 25	
Grease per lb.	0 06	...	Made on the Island.
Graton do.	0 06	...	Do. do.

E. PAKENHAM BROOKS,
Stipendiary Magistrate.

List of articles for sale at Diego Garcia Plantation shop, 1875.

have been rudimentary. The labourers were reported to have a great fondness for the castor oil administered. Generally the state of health of the labourers was good. Even some of the maladies which led to admission to the sick-bays or giving days off work were attributed by the management to malingering and too much strong liquor.

The population of Diego Garcia fluctuated between 350 and 550 during this period, with additional labour being imported as necessary. The birthrate on the islands was low. There remained a great imbalance between the sexes with women rarely constituting more than 20 per cent. Visitors frequently commented on this, attributing 'the sad state of morality prevailing to the inequality of the members of the sexes. Marriage is unknown and all the women appear to live in a state of concubinage.'[3]

Occasional though they were, the visits to Diego Garcia by British officials, either Special Commissioners such as Commander E. Hardinge of HMS *Persian* or, from 1864, by District Magistrates, such as J. H. Ackroyd and E. Pakenham Brooks, were not perfunctory efforts. Their standard directive from the Governor of Mauritius was threefold: to ensure that no one had been brought to the island against his or her own will, that no one was being kept there against his or her will, and that no one was being treated with cruelty or oppression or illegally detained. They probed with surprising intrusiveness into the island's affairs and their painstaking reports give fascinating glimpses of life on the island. They clearly saw it as their duty to guard against tyrannous behaviour on behalf of the management, which could all too easily have sprung up. They were not slow to upbraid and punish any such manifestations. Pakenham Brooks, who paid a visit as Special Magistrate in 1875, handed out sizable fines both to an under-manager at Point Marianne for striking a labourer and to James Spurs, the Manager at East Point, for unjustifiably imprisoning three labourers without sufficient cause. The management at Point Marianne and Minni Minni were also instructed to provide sick-bays for their workforce. Prices and weights and measures in the Company's shops were carefully checked and the labourers' accommodation, the hospital and the jail measured to ensure that they fulfilled minimum specifications.

The labourers were not slow in coming forward with complaints against their employers which mainly related to rations and hours of work. This was not always to their advantage. In one case, a labourer was fined for bringing a frivolous and unfounded complaint. There were also disputes between the labourers to adjudicate, usually relating to petty thefts and assaults but occasionally involving suicide and murder. Pakenham Brooks had to investigate one such 'atrocious crime' committed by Janvier, a 'Malagash', that is, a native of Madagascar, who apparently acted as some sort of voodoo doctor. According to the allegations he had 'bewitched' a pregnant woman called Laure, and in presiding at her delivery succeeded not only in killing the unfortunate woman but her twin babies as well. Pakenham Brooks went so far as to exhume the body but the state of decomposition was too advanced. The accused and witnesses were sent to Port Louis for the trial, where it is interesting to note that the Magistrate found Janvier not guilty.

Various attempts were made in the mid-nineteenth century to diversify the economy by introducing new crops and livestock. Maize or Indian corn, cotton, tobacco and citrus trees were tried and found to grow well. Captain Robert Moresby of the Indian Navy had planted breadfruit trees from Ceylon in 1837, which still survive at East Point. His survey of Diego Garcia incidentally produced charts which remained in use for a century and led to the naming of two promentories on the island after two of his officers, Lieutenants Simpson and Cust. Cattle, goats and sheep were also brought in for a while. Donkeys, introduced to drive the copra-grinding mills, became a permanent feature of the island from the 1840s. However, none of the agricultural experiments was pursued, probably because the well-established exploitation of the coconut, which now began to be cultivated systematically, continued to provide a steady and reliable income. In 1864, for revenue purposes, the estate at East Point was assessed as producing 51,000 gallons of coconut oil, Point Marianne 30,000 gallons, and Minni Minni 18,000 gallons.

Gilbert Bourne, who visited Diego Garcia a few years later under the auspices of the Royal Geographical Society, gave a comprehensive account of the process of extracting the oil:

Each palm will bear an abundance of coconuts for four or five years in succession, after which it remains comparatively unfruitful for another three years or more. The nuts when ripe fall on the ground, whence they are gathered by parties of men sent out in boats for the purpose. The daily task of each labourer is to collect, husk and deliver at the habitation 350 coconuts per diem. This is performed in a surprisingly short space of time when the nuts have not to be carried far by boat. Each party of men is in charge of a commander or sarang, who measures out a piece of ground on which each labourer is to work. The labourer collects the required number of coconuts into a heap, and then sticking a short broad-bladed spear into the ground, he takes each coconut, spits it upon the spear, and in a couple of wrenches has stripped off the husk and thrown the nut on one side.

On their arrival at the habitation the nuts are counted on the beach, and delivered to the women whose duty it is to break them and extract the kernel. The daily task of each woman is to break 1300 coconuts in the day, but I am told that they are able to break as many as 2500 in ten hours. The kernels, which are now known as copra, are then exposed to the sun in heaps, to allow an incipient fermentation setting in, but are carefully protected from the rain by a sort of pent-house on wheels, which can be run over the heaps at a minute's notice. After an exposure of two or three days, 250lbs of copra are delivered to each mill, this being the amount which each mill-labourer is required to grind daily; from it about 30 gallons of oil are produced. The mills used are of a most primitive pattern. The body of the mill is a hollow cylinder of hard wood, in which an upright beam of the same material is made to rotate, the motive power being supplied by three or four donkeys harnessed to a long horizontal beam, which is connected to the upright by a chain, and is weighted at the far end by two or three large lumps of coral. The copra is put in at the top of the cylinder, and the oil escapes by a hole at the bottom. The oil is merely strained through cloths and allowed to settle for a few days, after which it is run off into large vats, and is ready to be collected in casks and shipped for export. All the oil is exported to Mauritius by the oil company's ship, which calls three times a year at Diego Garcia.[4]

So well known were the Chagos for their principal product that they became known as the 'Oil Islands'. The middle of the century must have been a prosperous one for the coconut oil industry. Several of the most substantial buildings surviving in the East Point Plantation have the date 1864 inscribed on them. At that time on the other side of the world, the American Civil War was raging.

VIII

The Coaling
Station Interlude

The 1880s saw an intrusion of the outside world into Diego Garcia unparalleled until the establishment of the permanent naval facilities in the 1970s. The introduction of steam ships, which increasingly replaced the old sailing ships from the 1860s, gave rise to the need to establish strategically placed coaling stations along their routes. The newly constructed Suez Canal opened in 1869. For the routes to Australia and the Far East, Diego Garcia in the centre of the Indian Ocean seemed ideally situated. As Lionel Cox, Acting Procurator-General of Mauritius, noted:

> the advantages of Diego Garcia as a coaling station are now evidently well recognised ... There is little doubt that situated as this is on the straight line between the entrance to the Red Sea and Cape Leeuwin (on the South west Coast of Australia), and possessing a good harbour, it will become more and more important.[1]

In 1882 the Orient and Pacific Steam Navigation Company relocated its coaling station for the Australia run from Aden to Diego Garcia. Messrs Lund and Company also established itself. Traffic built up and by the second half of 1883 there were coaling visits by 34 large steamers as well as by two Royal Navy warships. Lund and Company, whose agent was George Worsell, kept its coal on hulks off East Point and ashore there. The coal was sold for £2 10 shillings a ton and was hauled by labourers hired from the plantation.

The Orient Company appointed James Spurs, the former manager of East Point, as its permanent agent. He, with characteristic energy, set about bringing in the latest technology for its operations. The Company's coal was kept mostly on hulks, initially off Minni Minni and later in the lee of Barton Point, accounting for the name Orient Bay, but some also on shore at East Point. To transfer the coal to the visiting ships 12 iron lighters were brought in sections and assembled on the spot by artisans from Greece and England. A 35 horse-power tug was used to pull the lighters and the coal was hoisted into the ship by special steam appliances. Spurs based himself on East Island and his work force on Middle Island which was leased to the Orient Company. The remains of the buildings, wells and some of the equipment can still be seen on these islands. The latter included 'a large condensing apparatus which will furnish a sufficient supply of wholesome distilled, filtered and aerated water for the use of the manager and labourers.'[2]

The need for safe navigation of the lagoon by ships calling to coal led to the carrying out of an accurate and detailed survey in 1885 by Captain the Honourable E. P. Vereker, in HMS *Rambler*, after which the bay north of Minni Minni is named. There was also a plan to place lighthouses at Horsburgh Point and West Island. This was never implemented, though temporary lights on posts were rigged up.

Labour proved a problem. Initially 40 Somalis were brought from Port Said but they proved unreliable and troublesome, and were sent back. They were replaced by labour from Mauritius who did not prove entirely satisfactory either, and there was an abortive project to recruit Chinese instead. Imported labour seems to have been behind a near insurrection in 1883 described by Bourne when the residence of the manager at East Point, Mr Leconte, was besieged by a mob of about 30 men armed with knives and clubs who threatened his life.

> Luckily for him they were as cowardly as they were insolent, and he was able to keep them at bay by presenting a revolver, until he had succeeded in reducing them to a more reasonable state of mind.[3]

The crews and passengers of the visiting ships, carrying such diverse elements as migrants to Australia and Moslem Javanese pilgrims on their way to Mecca, also contributed to the Wild West atmosphere on Diego Garcia in the 1880s. Those on board the ships were not meant to disembark, for quarantine reasons, but this instruction was often ignored, causing havoc ashore. In February 1884 for example, Captain Raymond of the *Windsor Castle*, while in a drunken fit

> landed at East Point with 16 men with loaded guns; had the Union Jack hoisted on the top of a tree in front of the manager's house; paraded his men; had a volley fired at the house (fortunately unoccupied), patrolled about, informed the manager that he had taken possession of the island in the name of the British Government and appointed the Manager Mr Leconte in writing as Lieutenant Governor.[4]

The plantation workers too became infected with the general air of indiscipline. They were induced on board the ships and administered strong drink. There were attempts to desert, some of them successful. Two labourers stowed away on an Orient Company steamer and got as far as Port Said in Egypt.

Visiting British officials noted the deterioration in law and order with concern and were not themselves immune from its manifestations. The memorably named Mr Ivanoff Dupont was exasperated by the lack of respect shown him by the labourers of the Orient Company on Middle Island but, especially as some of those concerned were said to be armed, decided that discretion was the better part of valour. He reported somewhat plaintively:

> the attitude of these men was impertinent and provoking to the extreme, and they would have met with severe punishment had I the means of enforcing my judgement. But I had not the assistance of policemen, which I would have asked for before leaving Mauritius had I known the state of insubordination in which I found some of the labourers of the Orient Company, and I considered it wiser to let them go unpunished.[5]

As a result of Dupont's report, the authorities in Mauritius concluded there was a need for an officer stationed in Diego Garcia 'who will make all, high or low, feel that they are living under the authority of the Queen and that differences are not to be adjusted by means of sticks and knives and revolvers'.[6] In response to the unprecedented threats to law and order it was decided in 1885 to set up a police post at Minni Minni at the surprisingly large contemporary cost of £1000 and with a sizable complement of an inspector, a Mr V. A. Butler, sergeant and six constables. The inspector's request for a steam launch was however turned down by the Colonial Secretary on the grounds of expense. Indeed the cost of the police operation and the disinclination of the Imperial Government, the authorities in Mauritius and the companies operating in the island to pay for it led to the withdrawal of the police presence in 1888. Although Special Constables were appointed as needed, it was not until 1973 that regular British policemen were reintroduced to Diego Garcia.

In any case, the use of the island as a coaling station did not last beyond the end of the decade. The introduction of larger ships with a longer range rendered the use of Diego Garcia superfluous. In 1888 a visiting official, Mr A. Boucherat, reported that:

> it does not seem at all certain that Lund's coaling com-

pany will continue its operations at Diego Garcia. The Orient Company no longer have their coaling station on East Island. The Agent has left for Colombo, having sold the greater part of the stock.[7]

What happened to any remains of the coal stocks is unclear. Perhaps some of it litters the floor of the lagoon.

After this shortlived brush with the developing modern world, the island returned to its sleepy existence as a plantation economy. Developments of local importance included the erection of a chapel at East Point in 1895, and the building of a light railway, whose remains can still be seen, to carry produce to the new jetty. More significantly, in the early 1900s coconut oil gave way to copra as the main product. This was partly because oil was falling into disuse as a means of lighting and partly because of the introduction of new and more efficient techniques to dry copra using a combination of solar power and furnaces fed by husks of coconuts.

IX

The *Emden* Incident

Diego Garcia's next brush with the wider world came at the outbreak of the First World War. Anglo-German naval rivalry dating from the last decades of the nineteenth century had its manifestations in the Indian Ocean as elsewhere on the globe. The expansion of German naval power posed a challenge to the established British maritime ascendancy which caused similar anxiety to that occasioned to the West by the world-wide Soviet build-up at sea in the 1960s and 1970s.

With naval bases a key preoccupation the Royal Navy watched with growing unease as German ships, both merchant and naval, began to visit Diego Garcia. The inhabitants became increasingly accustomed to the sight of the world's warships anchored in the lagoon. In the two-year period from 1888 to 1890 a German, an Austrian and a Russian warship, as well as four Royal Navy ships, visited the island. In 1899 there was a call by the German ships SMS *Bismarck* and SMS *Marie*, closely followed by HMS *Hampshire* and HMS *Empress of Russia*.

There was talk of fortifying the island, though nothing came of it. As Bourne had remarked earlier, 'how this is to be done and what use it would be to fortify an island ten feet high, which might be commanded by a ship sailing outside it, I am at a loss to know'.[1] Even had Diego Garcia been fortified, it would have made no difference when the German Warship SMS *Emden,* accompanied by the coaler *Buresk* entered the lagoon at dawn on 9 October 1914. The First World War had begun more than two months before but news of this had not yet reached the island, which had no wireless installed and had received its last visit from Mauritius three months earlier.

The *Emden* was a 3500-ton light cruiser equipped with ten 4.2 inch guns, torpedoes and carrying a crew of 361 men commanded by Captain von Müller. The ship had found itself stranded by the outbreak of war with the German Squadron on the China station. After escorting German supply ships to the Caroline Islands in the Pacific, then German territory, the *Emden* was detached in mid-August 1914 by Admiral Graf Spee to prey on allied shipping in the Indian Ocean, including the convoys bringing troop reinforcements and food to the Mother Country from the Empire. Such was the daring and resourcefulness of the *Emden* that her exploits attracted the admiration even of her opponents, including Winston Churchill, then First Lord of the Admiralty.

Having passed through the Straits of Molucca, the *Emden* coaled in neutral waters in the Netherlands East Indies and rigged an additional, false funnel in order to change her appearance. She then proceeded to the Bay of Bengal where she captured 13 allied merchant ships in the space of a fortnight. Shipping in the entire area was paralysed. The fox was in the chicken coop. On her way to a new hunting area on the other side of India, the *Emden* bombarded fuel tanks near Madras, causing enormous damage and provoking panic among the local population. Around the Maldives she intercepted three more ships but, learning from radio interception that pursuing Royal Navy ships were approaching, she decided to make herself scarce.

After several months at sea, the *Emden* badly needed to overhaul her engines, clean mussels and weed, which were reducing her speed, from the bottom of the ship and to make other repairs. According to the memoirs of one of her officers, Lieutenant the Prince of Hohenzollern, a relative of the German Emperor, Diego Garcia, 'a miniature fairyland of coral banks covered in high palms and a sheltered bay which cannot be seen from the sea'[2] offered an ideal haven. As the *Emden* made its way south across the Equator, the crew made what repairs they could at sea, exercised the ship's guns against a target towed behind the *Buresk* and, perhaps in anticipation of opposition ashore, practised infantry tactics with rifles and machine guns.

After the *Emden* and the *Buresk* had dropped anchor in the lagoon, a boat put out from the shore bearing the assistant manager of the plantation, Mr W. Suzor. He was brought into the wardroom and in Lieutenant Hohenzollern's words 'made very good practice with the iced whisky and soda. For us the conversation became interesting from the moment we recognised that this manager and the inhabitants had no idea there was a war on in the world.'[3] The assistant manager readily accepted the story that the German ship was involved in a major naval exercise involving other navies but was understandably eager for news of the outside world. According to Lieutenant Hohenzollern, the ships' officers embroidered selective information such as the death of Pope Pius X, with 'fairy stories'. When the plantation manager, Mr W. Cummins, joined his assistant, however, he proved more inquisitive and searching in his questions, demanding to know why the ship was in such a state. Captain von Müller assured him that this was because of a frightful storm which had been encountered, and the manager's mind too was put at rest.

Meanwhile the *Emden*'s crew manhandled on board 1000 tons of coal from the *Buresk*. By flooding some of the watertight compartments, they were able to cant the vessel, tilting each end successively into the air, and so to clean off the encrustations from the ship's bottom. They also agreed to repair the manager's motorboat for him and received in return welcome fresh food in the shape of a live pig, fish and fruit. Not wishing to be under any obligation to their albeit unaware enemies, the crew reciprocated with wine, spirits and cigars. 'I think the Diego Garcia people never had such noble givers as guests', commented Lieutenant Hohenzollern.[4] After two days the Germans left, in too much of a hurry to wait for the lobsters the islanders were collecting for them. The Germans' instinct was right, for eight hours later pursuing Royal Navy warships entered the lagoon. A major naval battle at Diego Garcia, like that off the Falklands a few weeks later when the *Emden*'s former companions from the German China Squadron were sunk, had only just been avoided.

From the Chagos the *Emden* steamed north to the Maldives again where it intercepted seven more merchantmen before vanishing into the eastern Indian Ocean, only to appear suddenly at the port of Penang in Malaya. Here a Russian cruiser and a French destroyer were sunk in short order by her torpedoes and guns. But the *Emden*'s luck finally ran out when it tried a similar exploit to that at Diego Garcia at the British-ruled Cocos-Keeling Islands. Here there was a wireless station which was able to send off a signal, 'Strange ship off entrance', before it could be silenced. Engaged by the cruiser HMAS *Sydney*, which was escorting a convoy of Australian troops nearby, the *Emden* was outgunned, rapidly set ablaze and beached on 9 November 1914, exactly one month after its visit to Diego Garcia. The surviving members of the crew were made prisoner but, by order of Winston Churchill, Captain von Müller and his officers were allowed to keep their swords as a tribute to their daring, gallantry and respect for the rules of naval warfare.

X

Partir C'est Mourir un Peu: Life Between the Wars

In the 1930s and early 1940s a French Roman Catholic priest Father Roger Dussercle, a native of Normandy, paid a number of visits to the Chagos which he described in several books which he had published at his own expense in Mauritius. Photographs taken by a British soldier Sergeant Barnett during the Second World War show Dussercle as bluff, well-built, with a black bushy beard and sporting a pith-helmet. He was sent by the Archbishop Leen of Port Louis to minister to, as the Archbishop put it, 'those poor souls who have till now been more or less abandoned'. Writing in 1846, Pridham had described the spiritual state of the inhabitants as follows: 'there exists no means of instruction among these poor people, either religious or secular; they had scarcely an idea of a Supreme Being.'[1] Other nineteenth-century visitors frequently made similar observations. Forty years after Pridham, Bourne observed: 'no priest is resident on the island, nor is there any arrangement for religious or other education.'[2] As Pridham had commented, 'Here then is a field, however small or obscure, for some missionary.'[3]

Previous pastoral visits to the islands seem to have been few and far between before Dussercle's mission. The first recorded is by the intrepid Bishop Vincent, the Anglican Bishop of Mauritius, who made the difficult voyage to the Chagos in 1859. He found there 'a good proportion of Protestants', including some who could repeat the Lord's Prayer and the Creed in English, and he carried out several baptisms. The Bishop thought the islands 'a most promising field of labour'.[4] There were at least two visits by Roman Catholic priests in 1875 and 1884. It is doubtful whether the nuances of denominations made much sense to the islanders, although one of Dussercle's aims was to eliminate Protestantism from the island, a goal foiled by the stubbornness of one particular woman who resisted all his blandishments to convert.

Setting sail from Port Louis in the 380-ton three-masted barque the *Diego* in November 1933, Father Dussercle took 15 days to reach the islands. His arrival, as he stepped ashore from the motor boat *Marshal Foch*, caused, like all visits from the outside, a great stir. He found a community and a way of life in many respects little changed from earlier accounts written in the nineteenth century. About 60 per cent of the population were now 'children of the islands' or *Ilois*, who had been born and bred there. They wore a 'national dress' of striped material, patterned like that of mattress covers, and spoke a Creole similar to that of Mauritius. Dussercle describes them as like big children, simple and amenable. Their diet consisted of rice, pork, chicken and fish, with wine and tobacco as simple luxuries. With all their immediate needs taken care of, they were, according to Dussercle, 'the happiest people in the world from the material point of view'.[5]

Dussercle described his pastoral duties in lyrical terms. He took the children through their catechism under the shade of a giant takamaka tree at Point Marianne, and on the beach at East Point in order to catch the breeze. He administered

First Communion to young and old confirmants. He celebrated Christmas midnight mass under the stars at an altar
decorated with palm fronds and garlands of flowers which
was set up near the jetty at East Point. Rich, strong island
voices sang familiar carols such as 'Come all ye faithful' and
'Midnight, Christians'. Dussercle preached good sermons in
Creole, drawing on his deep familiarity with the islanders'
language and folk stories. He warned of the danger of death
which came suddenly 'like a thief at the gate', or like 'brother
hare', and which, if not prepared for, could lead to an eter-
nity in hell, stewing in hot spice and salt. After the service
the entire island population processed round the settlement
from lagoon-side to ocean-side.

However, there were what Dussercle regarded as persistent
moral problems, especially a deplorable tendency for couples
to live together without benefit of formal marriage. The local
description of this practice was to be 'married from behind
the kitchen'. Dussercle said that in that case these were the
'Devil's kitchens'. He spent much of his visits to the island
trying to persuade couples to regularise their situations but
with only limited success. It may be that the women, who
were still in a minority, found it an advantage not to be
bound to one man. Apart from this, it was, as before, the
labour recruited from outside who were seen by Dussercle as
a disruptive influence, possibly because they were less
inclined to accept the paternalistic system run by the Oil
Company.

As before, copra was exported three or four times a year
to Mauritius for processing. But some coconut oil was still
produced for local use by primitive mills driven by donkey-
power. Although some people lived at Point Marianne and
Minni Minni, all copra processing had been concentrated at
East Point. The set-up at East Point was typical of the other
'Oil Islands', with a manager's residence or *château*, a chapel,
which was built in its present form during this period after
the existing one was flattened by a tree in a storm in October
1932, a shop, copra drying sheds, an oil mill, boatsheds, a
sail-maker's shed, a workshop, hospital and jail. All these

buildings can still be seen at the East Point Plantation site. The Manager's private chapel behind the Plantation House was reconsecrated by Dussercle in 1933, as a stone set in the wall proclaims. The jail contained four cells. During Dussercle's second visit, three of these were occupied by two men, who had killed a donkey to use its skin for a drum, and a young woman who had been cheeky to a supervisor.

A typical labourer's hut was divided into rooms by partitions made of coconut fronds. In the sleeping quarters were straw mattresses, raised above the ground on short stilts. Tattered clothes were scattered on the floor or hung up by strings. The living room was plastered with picture postcards and greeting cards, often with representations of couples in amorous poses. On cheap shelves were knick-knacks, decorative plates and occasionally a cheap and scratchy gramophone. Finally, there were drums for use in dancing, which was presumably what the inhabitants of the jail had in mind for the wretched donkey's skin.

Sports days and picnics were part of island life when it came to holidays and other celebrations. Dussercle records a Christmas afternoon of donkey races, sack races, bobbing for pieces of bread on strings, tug of war and swimming competitions. Dances were also held to the music of accordions, mouth organs and a sort of one-stringed harp. A dance which gave Dussercle particularly grave cause for concern was that typical of the islands, the *Séga*. No doubt because of the Mozambican origin of many of the islanders, this dance seems to have come from central Mozambique, where a similar dance exists to this day.[6] It was regarded by Dussercle and other European visitors as a throwback to African roots and too wild and abandoned for civilized tastes, accompanied by wild drumming, stamping of feet and suggestive movements as well as generous infusions of rum. The dance, held around a fire on a beach or in a clearing, went on for several hours and became increasingly frenzied and reportedly often ended in fornication. The islanders were very attached to the dance. An attempt by a manager in the Salomons to ban *Séga* in 1937 led to an insurrection. A more decorous version of the dance is still performed in Mauritius.

The *Séga* was not the only African survival which caused Dussercle concern. Distinctly non-Christian death cere-monies, intended to ensure that the ghost would not haunt the living, continued to be practised. Reports of these had cropped up before. In October 1886 a certain Louis Fidèle had been imprisoned for 'practising witchcraft in the Cem-etery'. Dussercle described these practices as 'savage, barbar-ous and often bestial . . . such as one would only expect to find in the middle of Africa'. According to him the rites, which went on for eight days after the death, involved 'orgies, disgusting talk, witchcraft, casting spells, hellish invocations, devilish incantations, lascivious dancing, immoral getups, frenetic leaping off coconut trees on to the roofs of huts, and all accompanied by revolting acts committed on the corpse'.[6] Having given this lurid description Dussercle said that he was not prepared to give more detail in order not to shock normal sensibilities!

Dussercle made the Chagos his special field of labour and, despite suffering shipwreck with the *Diego* on Eagle Island in June 1935, continued to serve the inhabitants of Diego Garcia through periodic visits up to and during the Second World War. He also ministered to the military garrison stationed on Diego Garcia during the war and presided at the funerals of those soldiers who are buried at Point Marianne cemetery.

Dussercle loved the islands and their people. As he quoted on his departure, 'Partir c'est mourir un peu' (to leave is to die a little).[7] Many have felt the same on leaving Diego for the last time.

XI

Outpost of Empire: Diego Garcia and the Second World War

During the Second World War, as in the First, German raiders preying on allied merchant shipping entered the Indian Ocean from time to time. The pocket battleship *Scheer* sank ten ships in the first three months of 1941. The raider *Thor*, a disguised armed merchantman equipped with its own aeroplane, was active in the central Indian Ocean to the south of the Chagos from May to August 1942, but did not try to emulate the *Emden* by visiting Diego Garcia.

However, in early 1942 a threat of a different order began to develop from the East. In December 1941, shortly after the attack on Pearl Harbor, the sinking by Japanese aircraft of the battleship HMS *Prince of Wales* and the cruiser HMS *Repulse* in the South China Sea was followed by the fall of

Malaya, Singapore and the Netherlands East Indies (now Indonesia) in January to March 1942. Japanese armies also advanced through Burma to the gates of India and seized the Andaman Islands in the Bay of Bengal. The Indian Ocean was now wide open to Japanese naval attack, both surface and submarine.

In response to the Japanese threat, the British hurriedly developed a chain of naval and air bases and refuelling stations between Ceylon and the coast of Africa in early 1942. The huge natural harbour provided by Addu Atoll at the southern point of the Maldive Islands, about 400 miles north of Diego Garcia, was developed in conditions of great secrecy as an alternative base to Ceylon for the British Eastern fleet and was code-named Port T. If, as was feared at the time, the Japanese had invaded Ceylon, it is possible the fleet would have been forced to move farther south to Diego Garcia. As it was, steps were taken to provide defences for Diego Garcia which was given the code-name Port 2Y. Along with the Seychelles and Mauritius, Diego Garcia was to serve as a refuelling and minor base for naval craft and flying boats. A battery of 6-inch guns was installed on the north-west tip of the island to command the entrance to the lagoon. These guns can still be seen at Cannon Point.

We have a snapshot of life in wartime Diego Garcia because of an autobiographical book, *Only the Sun Remembers*, and a collection of poems, 'Military Honours', written by a young Scottish Royal Marine Captain, J. Alan Thompson, who served on the island in early 1942 to supervise the installation of the gun battery. Although Marines embarked on British ships no doubt visited the island from the eighteenth century onwards, the detachment commanded by Thompson was the first to be actually stationed on Diego Garcia. The two ex-naval guns which they installed were brought in a merchant ship, the SS *Clan Forbes*. There were inevitable accidents. A young sergeant was knocked overboard on to a landing craft and died of head injuries. His body was buried at sea. Thompson may have had this in mind in his poem 'War to the Atoll', where he wrote:

... our once laughing friends
Snug in their taut neat canvas shrouds,
Tumble down green alleyways of weeds
Gnawed by the passing shark ... [1]

The guns were pulled to their positions by tractors and winched into place. During this process teeth in the winching gear slipped and a Marine Morris was struck severely on the forehead by an iron winching handle. Against the odds he survived this appalling injury after convalescence in the hospital at East Point. The Marines suffered from more banal afflictions, including prickly heat and intense skin rashes and blisters which rendered movement miserable and made them dream of the cold winds of Norway where they had served earlier in the war.

Homesick and separated from his newly married bride, Captain Thompson drew a rather jaundiced view of Diego Garcia, which he described as 'an empty fort in the sea desert ... life years away from the world'. He complained of the heat – 'the sun burned nearer to the earth in Chagos' – and the tropical storms – 'squalls of ungovernable fury' drenching the 'hungry, shallow earth' – and the jungle – 'a useless maze of vegetation, the dense palm growth, weird bushes, the impenetrable thickets, the wooden walls of ... banyan, the giant hardwood trees'.[2]

Thompson was scarcely more complimentary about the inhabitants who, in an echo of previous descriptions, he said were 'normally carefree, good humoured, rich in laughter; but unforeseeably vicious, sullen, heat-tempered [sic] and passionate, wildblooded, uncertain, vitriolic, ignorant. Dirty, guileless and cunning, pleasantly manageable or dangerously intractable, ready knived, cowardly, mob conscious'.[3] The women clearly disturbed him with their open sexuality. He described an encounter with women returning from the coconut plantations who, as would be said today, sexually harassed him by standing in his path and baring their breasts.

The Mauritian under-manager at East Point at this time was called Bertillon. According to Thompson, he was a

'Picasso man' and resembled a dirty white toadstool in his extraordinarily wide-brimmed sun helmet, which he wore day and night. Bertillon had not left the island for 14 years but dreamed of returning to Mauritius one day. He was on bad terms with the over-manager, Malbois, who lived at Point Marianne with two women, one described as his wife and the other as her sister.

Bertillon drove a Ford truck on the track which ran around the island, but the quickest way then to travel from East Point to Point Marianne was by boat across the lagoon.

Bertillon took the Marines out on a night expedition to look for edible crabs by the light of torches, duly terrifying them with talk of giant crustaceans which snapped like bull-dogs. He also took them fishing in the lagoon and on the open sea, where tuna and shark were easily hooked. Thompson described Diego as:

> the fisherman's paradise; the incredible Valhalla where all lies come true, where the two exaggerating arms cannot span the fish he caught; where there is neither doubt nor hope but only the certainty of catching fish until his arm is tired or the line snaps . . . Fishing in paradise, in the kind waters of greedy and ignorant fish: dream fish, fish weighing ten, twenty, fifty, one hundred pounds.[4]

Clearly little has changed in this respect as regards fishing in Diego Garcia.

Unlike Father Dussercle, Thompson was able, thanks to Bertillon who was rewarded with bottles of whisky, to observe from concealment a fully-fledged *Séga*. The event took place under a full moon in a clearing to the north of East Point. By the light of the moon and a fire, the participants drank rum and then danced to the quickening beat of the drums with increasing frenzy and sensuality. Thompson left a graphic account:

> As if automatons awakened the scene gradually stirred

into life, the toys moved stiffly in the shadows ... The
drums grew louder, quicker, the beat deepening to a
wild urgency ... slowly the rhythm and movement
increased; the dancers' bodies glistened and shone in
the heat ... couples paired and danced together ...
They danced closer, their bodies touching, rubbing ...
The endless drumming now a drug, the blood of the
living moment, burrowing into muscle and brain, throb-
bing in the body like an iron pulse, alive, dynamic.[5]

The upshot was very much as Father Dussercle had feared.
One can imagine the effect on the lovelorn Marines, far from
home.

Captain Thompson and his men left Diego Garcia in
March 1942 without regret. However, in his poetry and book
about his wartime experiences he left vivid descriptions of
the island, some of which have been quoted in earlier chap-
ters. The island was subsequently garrisoned by a mixed force
of British, Mauritian and Indian troops. The guns were
manned by men of the 1st and 25th Coast Batteries, Royal
Artillery, recruited in Mauritius. Indian forces stationed on
Diego Garcia included Pathans from the North West Frontier,
Sikhs of the Bombay Grenadiers and Goan Pioneers. The
graves of those who fell prey to diseases such as scrub typhus
during their lonely vigil can be seen at Point Marianne cemetery. An annual Remembrance Service is still held on 11
November at Point Marianne. Captain Thompson left a vivid
description of the funeral of one of these soldiers in his
poem 'Military Honours':

> ... the dead
> who passes in the breath defying heat,
> between the rigid, gasping trees,
> beneath a flag, and shaken by a lorry
> slowed for the damp uncaring feet
> that march with stolid step beside.
> Hard rifles glinting dully in the sun

shirts dark with sweat, the lifting glare,
each head annoyed because he died.[6]

Life was tough for the troops, with few pleasures, although
Sergeant Fred Barnett, then a 21-year-old fitter in the Royal
Artillery remembers some lighter moments, with his com-
rades and his pet Maltese poodle Charlie: the brewing of
home-made beer, the 'windfall' of bottles of gin buried on
the beach at East Point (where they may still lie), and the
incident in which the only two military trucks on the island
managed to collide on the island's only road.[7]

A detachment of Royal Air Force Catalina flying boats was
also stationed on Diego Garcia during the Second World
War. The Catalina was a versatile aircraft used for maritime
surveillance and attack, the forerunner of the P3s and Nim-
rods which now frequent the island. It had long endurance,
being able to operate within a range of 4000 miles for $17^1/_2$
hours without refuelling. It carried three machine guns and
a 2000 lb bomb load. It was a Catalina which spotted the
same Japanese fleet whose aircraft had raided Pearl Harbor,
on its way to mount a surprise attack on British naval bases
in Ceylon in early April 1942. With the warning provided,
the British air defences were able to give the Japanese a
bloody nose and the surface threat receded, although
Japanese submarines and surface raiders continued to range
widely in the Indian Ocean.

The 29th Advanced Flying Boat base on Diego Garcia was
at East Point, where there was also a wireless and a weather
station. These buildings still stand. Detachments from both
Nos 205 and 240 Squadrons RAF, based in Ceylon, were sent
to East Point. According to the Operations Record Book of
No. 205 Squadron RAF in July 1944, the 'facilities at Diego
Garcia are still very inadequate; insufficient personnel, insufficient marine craft and bad living conditions'. As regards
the last there were 'no recreational facilities, the billets for
NCOs were without lights, flies and mosquitoes abound and
conditions are not ameliorated by the existence in the camp
area of a copra yard and donkey stables'. The 'reluctant and

inefficient ministrations of a creole cook' did not help.[8] A visit by a Royal Navy frigate, and gin and tonics in its ward room, helped to raise spirits. Later, however, improvements were wrought including spraying against mosquitoes, the organisation of an operations room with plotting and situation boards, and the arrival of stores on a large Sunderland flying boat. The main role of the Catalinas on Diego Garcia was hunting for enemy submarines, searching for survivors from sunken merchant vessels and collecting meteorological data. There were also exercises familiar to present-day flyers; night circuits and landing, and bombing practice against floating targets.

A very tangible relic of the Royal Air Force presence on Diego Garcia is the remains of a Catalina which can be seen on the beach north of East Point pier, still well preserved nearly 50 years later because of its aluminium construction. Cyclones are very rare in the Chagos which lie between the southern cyclone belt which periodically devastates Mauritius and Rodrigues and the more northerly Indian Ocean cyclone belt. However, occasionally a maverick cyclone strikes the Archipelago. In 1901 a visiting official reported:

> I had always heard that no cyclone ever passed the neighbourhood of the Chagos Group but while I was at Diego Garcia we felt the effects of a very strong one which passed south of us, the barometer falling to 29.5. The wind blew very hard and squalls were very strong, one thousand to fifteen hundred coconut trees were destroyed.[9]

The same happened on the night of 15/16 September 1944. Forty miles per hour winds began to lash the island. There were four Catalinas at East Point at the time, two from 205 Squadron and two from 240 Squadron. As the winds rose in the course of the night, the two 240 Squadron aircraft broke from their moorings, and by dawn they were beached on the shore. The seaplane tender also beached and several other support craft sunk. In the course of the morning the two other aircraft from 205 Squadron began to drift and efforts to rescue the guards on board failed when the refuelling craft foundered and sank in the rough seas. Working in driving rain and sand and with debris from collapsing buildings blowing around them, Flying Officer Usherwood and Sergeant Gregory set out in the only craft that remained, a rowing dinghy, and managed to save those on board the Catalinas still afloat. The wind now veered and threatened to throw one of these on the pier. While all attention was concentrated on averting this disaster, one of the beached Catalinas swung beam on to the tide and was irreparably damaged by a palm tree. There it lies to this day. Several generations of island children must have played in the shell, imagining they were piloting a plane. Ironically enough, another of the infrequent storms that hit Diego Garcia chose to do so in September 1990, causing serious disruption to tented accommodation and stores when the United States Air Force was deploying to the island in connection with Operation Desert Storm.

Diego Garcia was never directly attacked during the Second World War, although dramatic events took place all around it, including the British landings in Madagascar in May 1942 to prevent its use by Japanese submarines. British forces were withdrawn from Diego Garcia after the Japanese surrender in South East Asia to Lord Mountbatten at Singapore on 12 September 1945. A visitor a few years later, F. D. Ommanney, wrote that it was strange to see what used to be the Operations Room at East Point with a large operational map still in place on the wall, RAF emblems and pin-up girls ogling at nothing in the dusty heat.[10] The nearest remaining British base in the area was 400 miles to the north at Gan at the southern tip of the Maldives, until the withdrawal of the RAF station there in 1976.

XII

The End of an Era

Sources of information about Diego Garcia become more vivid during the period between the end of the Second World War and the final closure of the plantations in 1971. In addition to written accounts, there are now numerous photographs and even a colour movie film. As a result we can form a clear view of life on the island as the plantation era drew to a close. Obviously the pattern of life had still changed little since the nineteenth century, an amazing and perhaps unique survival of 'Gone with the Wind' plantation life.

Sir Robert Scott was Governor of Mauritius and visited Diego Garcia as part of a wider tour of inspection of the 'Oil Islands' in October 1955. What might have been simply a routine chore by a senior Colonial Office official produced a minor literary masterpiece. Scott was clearly enchanted by the islands and some years later transformed the diary he had kept and the observations he had jotted down into *Limuria*, a masterly and beautifully written survey of their history and their then state.

Scott arrived at Diego Garcia in the corvette HMS *Killisport*. East Point Plantation was at the peak of its development, set in a crescent of lawns and flowering shrubs. Scott described

East Point as having 'the look of a French coastal village, miraculously transferred whole to this shore',[1] with the manager's *château*, the chapel, white-washed buildings, thatched cottages and even lamp-standards all grouped around a village green. A substantial portion of the then 680 population of the island turned out on the pier to welcome him, waving Union Jacks and creating a fête-like atmosphere. The visit of the Governor was a major event.

According to Scott, for every human being there was at least a score of other creatures, chickens, ducks, dogs, cats, donkeys, horses, pigs. And for each creature there were thousands of flies, which could blanket a horse to the extent of transforming it into a piebald. The smell of drying copra was everywhere. As Scott observed:

> the principal characteristic of Diego Garcia is a prodigal fecundity, with the useful forms of life continually under pressure from the useless. The vegetation thrusts, sprawls, creeps, intertwines and shoots upward and sideways.[2]

(This vegetable vigour is the bane of efforts currently under way to preserve the East Point Plantation in a recognisable form.) Among the trees acrobatic rats disported themselves like squirrels.

In Scott's day, there was a motorable track both up to Barton Point and round the bottom of the island. There were a number of hamlets scattered around both arms of the island with now forgotten names and even locations. To the north of Minni Minni were Balisage, Camp du Puits and North East Camp; between East Point and Point Marianne lay Barochois, Roches Pointes, and Port Dumoulin; and to the north of Point Marianne, Noroit. Scott describes the islanders as dour and hard-headed compared with those of the other 'Oil Islands'. Like their present-day successors in Diego Garcia, they played soccer with an obvious and noisy consciousness that the match was for real and in earnest.

There had been some diversification of production on the

island. Dried fish, and timber from the large hardwood trees such as the takamaka, were exported. And from the mid-1950s guano for fertiliser was dug at the north-west end of the island, carted to the shore by tractors, and loaded on to a ship by barge. Maize, or Indian corn, was also grown on quite a large scale.

But exploitation of the coconut continued to provide the staple crop. Seven thousand nuts were needed to produce 1 ton of copra which in turn produced 11 hundredweight of crude oil. The film referred to above was made by the Colonial Film Unit, probably during Scott's visit. In scenes remarkably reminiscent of Bourne's account a century before, it shows in colour what was essentially an eighteenth- and nineteenth-century plantation society functioning in the middle of the twentieth century. The labourers are seen collecting fallen coconuts which they speared with cutlasses and tossed with great skill and rapidity into large baskets carried on their heads. As in Bourne's day the coconuts were then husked among the coconut groves on a stake-like device stuck in the ground. From there the nuts were taken by donkey and horsedrawn carts to East Point where women were waiting to break them into pieces with pestles and then, with the help of children, to chop them into even smaller bits. These were then spread out to dry on large concrete beds which, in the event of rain, could be covered in a matter of moments by corrugated-iron shelters on wheels. Finally, the copra was dried in hot-air chambers heated from below by burning coconut husks. Most of the dried copra was then exported by boat to Mauritius for the extraction of oil for cooking and soap. However, a small amount of oil for local needs was produced on the spot in a primitive mill composed of a beam in a large metal drum propelled by donkey power. These mills can still be seen at East Point. What was left over after the oil had been extracted was known as 'poonac' and was fed to pigs and poultry.

The same film also shows a weather balloon being released at the meteorological station at East Point, still a key element in particular for cyclone forecasting in that pre-satellite age.

The film gives a glimpse of the range of physical types among the islanders, from African to Malagasy to Creole, as they went about their work, propelling punt-like craft in the lagoon with long poles, and hanging up octopuses to dry to provide a culinary feast.

Neither the islanders nor indeed Scott could have had any inkling that the plantation era was soon to end, although his book contains some prophetic remarks about the artificial nature of the small society on Diego Garcia and the uncertainty of its long-term viability. The imbalance in sexes, with women in a distinct minority, and a low birth-rate characteristic of marginal populations, persisted. The drift away from the island to the bright lights and wider prospects of Mauritius was quickening. The population fell by 50 per cent between 1952 and 1962. As a result, labour to help work the plantations had to be imported from the Seychelles. By the mid-1960s imported labour outnumbered those born in Diego Garcia by two to one. Previously in the history of the Chagos Group, other islands had been abandoned as a result of commercial decisions; Three Brothers in the 1850s and the Egmonts and Eagle Island as recently as the 1930s. The events soon to take place on Diego Garcia were therefore by no means unprecedented.

Dependent on a single major staple crop, the plantation economy on Diego Garcia was in any case vulnerable and its future doubtful. By the early 1960s, the copra industry was in serious decline world-wide. As Scott put it:

> a population was drafted to the lesser Dependencies in the first place because there was work for it there. It moved from group to group as opportunities for paid work expanded and contracted. It was not a natural island society, and even today [1960], it shows little inclination to exploit the natural bounties of the island.[3]

Certainly no community could have survived the closure of the plantations. So even had the outside world not again projected itself into the islands, the long-term continuance of the way of life there must have been in doubt. History sadly shows a catalogue of such evacuations elsewhere in the world; St Kilda in the North Atlantic off the Scottish coast for example, and perhaps eventually Pitcairn in the Pacific.

XIII

The
Establishment of
BIOT and the
Coming of the
Americans

Whatever the future might have held if the islands had been left to their own devices, the period 1965–76 saw a decisive transformation in the use of Diego Garcia. World politics and the demands of naval strategy were the catalysts.

The potential and actual military use of the island had been considered before. In the later nineteenth century, as mentioned earlier, this had been dismissed by Gilbert Bourne on the grounds that 'what use would it be to fortify an island ten feet high, which might be completely commanded by a ship sailing outside of it?'[1] As we have seen limited use had been made of Diego Garcia as a base for maritime reconnaissance in the Second World War. But now it was to achieve much greater significance militarily and as a result to become a name known around the world.

The 1960s saw a wave of decolonisation sweep the Indian

Ocean area, with Britain granting independence to the East African countries, Aden and Mauritius. The decade also witnessed the advance of communism, especially in South East Asia. These trends both threatened existing Western, primarily British, military facilities in the Indian Ocean region, and presented a growing challenge to Western interests. The USA began to turn its attention to the Indian Ocean and the adjacent areas of the Middle East and the Horn of Africa, particularly when Britain felt obliged for economic reasons to begin running down the military burden it had borne East of Suez for so long. The attraction to the USA of military facilities which were both politically and financially cost-free was obvious. For its part, Britain wished to continue to make a contribution to Western security interests by making territory available for defence purposes.

The germ of the idea of establishing a facility on one of the British-ruled islands in the Indian Ocean began to form in the early 1960s and bilateral discussions were initiated. A survey team made a visit to several islands in the area in 1964. Diego Garcia was selected as a suitable site at an early point, with its superb natural harbour and ample room for an airfield. Another possible choice, Aldabra, was ruled out for environmental reasons. Although the construction of any facilities was some way ahead, the British Government decided to detach the Chagos Archipelago, together with a number of other Indian Ocean islands – Aldabra, Farquhar and Des Roches – and establish them as a separate dependent territory on 8 November 1965. Although there was some controversy about it afterwards, at the time this was done with the full agreement of the Mauritian and Seychelles governments, which received substantial financial and material compensation for these remote atolls in which they showed little interest.

The words of the proclamation setting up the new territory read:

> Her Majesty, by virtue and in exercise of the powers in that behalf by the Colonial Boundaries Act 1895 . . . is

> pleased, by and on the advice of Her Privy Council, to order ... that the Chagos Archipelago ... shall form a separate colony which shall be known as the British Indian Ocean Territory.[2]

The fledgling Colony was a unique post-imperial creation, established at a time when the Union Jack was coming down in the rest of the world. It is interesting to note that a number of other names for the new territory were considered but discarded, including Limuria. It soon became generally known by its shortened form of BIOT.

The proclamation of 8 November 1965 also laid down that to govern the islands:

> there should be a Commissioner for the Territory who shall be appointed by Her Majesty ... under her Majesty's Sign Manual and Signet and shall hold office during her Majesty's pleasure.

The first BIOT Commissioner, a throwback to earlier nomenclature applied to visiting officials, was the Earl of Oxford and Asquith, who was already Governor of the Seychelles. The first Administrator Mr J. R. Todd, who was also Deputy Governor of the Seychelles, visited the islands in March 1967.

In 1966 Britain and the United States signed an agreement which still governs the use of Diego Garcia and the other islands of BIOT. This made the islands available to meet the defence needs of both Governments for 'an indefinitely long period'.[3] The initial period of the agreement was to run 50 years, that is, to the year 2016, and would be renewed automatically for a further 20 years unless either Government decided to give notice of termination at this point.

Despite the agreement in principle to develop Diego Garcia for defence purposes, events moved at a leisurely pace over the next few years and plantation life carried on. The population of the island in 1968 was 380. The Chagos Agalega Company of Seychelles had acquired the freeholds in 1962 from the long-standing Paris-based Société Huilière de Diégo et Péros. These were in turn bought out by the British Government in March 1967 for £1.1 million but the management continued in the hands of the company up to the final evacuation. A 500-ton cargo ship, the *Nordvaer* was acquired by the BIOT administration in July 1968 to ply between the Chagos and Mahé in the Seychelles, from which the territory was now effectively governed.

In June and July of 1967 a detailed hydrographic survey of the lagoon at Diego Garcia was carried out by Captain C. R. K. Roe, RN in HMS *Vidal*. In 1968 the United States Government formulated a specific proposal to develop what was described as an 'austere' communications station and associated airfield on the western side of Diego Garcia. However, there was a setback in December 1969 when Congress struck out the provision for this in the annual Appropriation Bill. In December 1970 Congress reversed itself and passed the Military Construction Bill containing an appropriation for Diego Garcia. An American reconnaissance team visited the island in January 1971, and the first 20-man advance party of the Naval Mobile Construction Battalion 40 of the U.S. combat engineers, the 'Seabees', who were to undertake the work arrived in March 1971.

This was by no means the first American presence in the area. There had been sufficient maritime activity in the Indian Ocean to justify the opening of a United States Consulate at Port Louis in then French-ruled Mauritius in 1794. With Yankee shrewdness, American ships conveyed from Mauritius in their neutral bottoms captured British merchandise taken by French privateers during the Revolutionary and Napoleonic wars. And throughout the nineteenth century, American whalers hunted the sperm whale in the waters around Diego Garcia, using the island as a source of water and fresh produce. Several were wrecked on the reefs around the Chagos. The print referred to in Chapter V shows the American brig *Pickering*, with Stars and Stripes flying, anchored off East Point in 1819, having rescued the crew of a Dutch ship, the *Admiral Evertson*.

The arrival of the Americans and the start of the construction work necessitated the closing of the plantation and the evacuation of the workers, whose legal position was that they were on contract, owned no immovable property and had no right of residence. As indicated earlier, the production of copra was ceasing to be an economic proposition and the new military environment was not conducive to the maintenance of the traditional way of life. For a short period, the old and new lifestyles co-existed but in October 1971 the last of the plantation workers and their families left after a final mass in Creole at East Point Chapel. The departure of those families who had worked and made their homes on Diego Garcia for generations was undoubtedly a traumatic experience. Some went to the northern islands of the Chagos group, the Salomons and Peros Banhos, where the copra plantations continued to be worked until 1973, and the rest to Agalega, the Seychelles and Mauritius.

Tractors, other vehicles and movable machinery were also taken away. Different fates awaited the various domestic animals. Caged birds including cardinals, yellow-vented bulbuls and finches were released into the wild. It would be interesting to know if any of these species survive to this day. Dogs and working donkeys were put down. But many donkeys had already escaped into the wild over the years and were left behind, as were a stallion and two mares which could not be captured and removed. At least one descendant of these horses, probably a mare, still ranges the jungle beyond East Point and is occasionally sighted like some island Loch Ness monster. Cats and chickens, some of which had also gone wild, were left behind as well. The ducks seem to have fallen prey to rats and cats because with their webbed feet they were unable to escape by roosting in the trees like the chickens. Although the islanders had long kept pigs, these must have been butchered and eaten since, unlike in the novel *Lord of the Flies*, no herds of wild pigs now roam this tropical island.

Most of the former islanders eventually ended up in Mauritius, where some, especially the older ones, undoubtedly found adjustment to a different way of life hard. In his novel,

A Lesser Dependency, Peter Benson describes graphically the experiences of a fictional island family after the evacuation. When hardships became known, the British Government provided financial assistance to help the islanders' resettlement, £650,000 in 1973 and a final *ex gratia* payment of £4 million in 1982, considerable sums in those days. The receipt to be signed for payments under this scheme contained the poignant undertaking never to return to the islands. Known to Mauritians, as are all people from the outlying islands, as the *Ilois* or islanders, the former inhabitants of Diego Garcia mostly live in a number of distinct villages in Mauritius. The younger generation are integrating well into Mauritian life but some of the older folk remain understandably nostalgic for their former way of life in 'les îles là-haut' – the islands up there – as they call the Chagos.

XIV

Footprint of
Freedom

The early 1970s were the heroic pioneer days of the
new military society on Diego Garcia. The construction project turned out to be the biggest ever undertaken by the Seabees (the United States Naval Construction
Corps). The first Seabees to arrive lived without air-condition-
ing in a tented camp and had little protection from the sun,
the rain, the coral dust and the spray. Many of the men were
veterans of Vietnam. The workday lasted between 10 and 12
hours and a 6-day week was standard. There were no formal
recreational facilities and leave off the island to Thailand was
granted only once during an eight-month tour of duty. As a
result a certain 'Wild West' atmosphere again permeated the
island as in the coaling station era nearly 100 years before.
The first US Commanding Officer was Commander Philip
Oliver, USN, appointed in early 1971.

Initial work included marking underwater obstructions,
installing temporary navigation aids and clearing beach areas,
so that equipment and material, all of which had to be
brought in from outside, could be landed. In the first year a
water and electrical distribution system, messing facilities,
refrigeration plant, storage sheds and jetty were installed.
The work was not without danger. A young Seabee, Charles

Cummins from Chicago, was fatally injured when the desalination plant boiler exploded in December 1971. A construction priority was the airfield which was sufficiently ready to receive the first C-130 flight in July 1971 on an interim 3,500-foot strip.

The departure of the last plantation manager, Mr Marcel Moulinie, necessitated the appointment of the first resident British representative, Lieutenant-Commander John Canter, RN, who landed on the temporary strip at night, in a thunderstorm, by the light of oil flares in September 1971.[1] Like his successors, Canter served as Commissioner's Representative, Her Majesty's Justice of the Peace, Post Master and Immigration Officer. In addition he acted as Air and Harbour Operations Officer and later as US Military Airlift Command (MAC) Liaison Officer, an unusual role for a British officer. Canter served the longest stint of any British Representative, until June 1974.

The first visit to the island by a BIOT Commissioner under the new dispensation was made in March 1972 by the then Governor of the Seychelles, Sir Bruce Greatbatch, who arrived in an RAF Hercules accompanied by the Administrator, John Todd. After the independence of the Seychelles in 1976, the Commissioner was based in London, with this job becoming coterminous with that of the head of the Department in the Foreign and Commonwealth Office responsible for the region. Another notable early visitor was the entertainer Bob Hope, who came with his wife and the then reigning Miss World to give a show on Christmas Day 1972. This visit, which involved a long and arduous journey, was much appreciated by the personnel on the island. Bob Hope visited the island again in 1982, when he found things a lot more civilized. This time he was accompanied by the Dallas Cowgirls, and the present VIP quarters were named in his honour.

By the beginning of 1973 the Naval Communications Station, comprising three sites, two at the north-western end of the island and one at the southern tip, was ready for operation. The commissioning ceremony took place on 20

March 1973 in the presence of Captain R. L. Thorson, USN, Deputy Commander, Naval Communications Command, with Commander C. E. Hamilton, USN, assuming charge of the Station. Until the early 1980s, the Communications Station was manned on an integrated basis by both Royal Navy and United States Navy personnel.

The first BIOT Police Officer was appointed at the same time. The need arose partly from the arrival of civilians subject to BIOT law in the form of personnel from Taiwan brought in to blast part of the reef to allow construction of a jetty. The enlarged British party established the first British Club in a former plantation building, the Busher's, that is, the Foreman's, Hut from the Old North West Plantation, which can still be seen on the side of the road near the sports field. From the start it proved a popular resort for all nationalities on the island. The present British Club dates from 1980 and has already acquired considerable character, reminiscent of an English pub transplanted to the tropics.

No sooner was the Communications Station in operation than developments in South-East Asia and the Middle East and the build up of Soviet military presence, including that at the mouth of the Red Sea in Aden and Berbera, led the United States to submit a proposal to the British Government to expand the facilities on Diego Garcia. The proposal was to establish a Naval Support Facility consisting of a fleet anchorage, enlarged airfield and associated services, in order to provide central logistic support to forces operating in the Indian Ocean. An Exchange of Notes between the two Governments in February 1976 formalised the agreement.[2] In the context of the Cold War further development of the island for military purposes attracted strong objections from the Soviet Union as well as from some states of the region, and was not without controversy domestically in Britain and the United States as well, with allegations that an 'aggressive nuclear base' was being inserted into the Indian Ocean.

Work on the expansion began forthwith. The massive task of enlarging the runway to 12,000 feet, constructing a pier by which large ships could berth and building a large fuel storage area, as well as accommodation and facilities for the additional personnel, was begun by the US 30th Naval Construction Regiment and handed over to a civilian contractor in 1981. The Naval Support Facility itself was commissioned on 1 October 1977. Its first Commanding Officer was Captain B. Andrews, USN, who also assumed the position of US island commander. At this point the resident population of the island was about 1,300 men, of whom about half were engaged in construction. Women were still not permitted to serve on the island at that time, although there were some visits by female personnel and occasional yachtswomen. Four Australian women from a yacht appeared on the beach one day stark naked, to the consternation of the authorities and the delectation of the men.[3]

A considerable effort was put into ensuring that the expansion was carried out in such a way as to cause the least harm to the environment of the island which, as described earlier, is rich in coraline, marine and avian life. The 1976 Agreement reiterated the clause of its predecessor in 1972, governing the use of the communications facility, that as far as possible the activities of the Naval Support Facility and its personnel should not interfere with the flora and fauna of Diego Garcia. Successive British representatives took a close interest in the environmental impact of construction work. Commander John Topp, RN, who served from 1984 to 1986, produced a scholarly work on the flora of the island which was published by the Smithsonian Institution. Ordinances were published for the protection of wildlife, including green and hawksbill turtles and coconut and land crabs, and a bird sanctuary was established on East Island at the mouth of the lagoon. Rigorous steps were taken to avoid pollution of the lagoon and the sub-soil. There is an environmental plan on whose implementation annual reports are submitted to the British authorities. The British Government also reserves the right to grant access to members of scientific parties wishing to carry out research on Diego Garcia, and there have been a number of such visits. Since October 1991 commercial fishing has been regulated in a 200-mile zone around the Chagos.

By the mid-1980s, the naval facility was much as it exists today. The logistic support merchant ships of the pre-positioning squadron stationed at Diego Garcia arrived in July 1980. The US Navy P3 air surveillance squadron was stationed there permanently in 1985. And US Marines and Royal Marines have served side by side since 1981 to provide security. From 1981 further construction work and maintenance of the existing facilities was undertaken by civilian contractors from joint Anglo-American consortia. The population, military and civilian, from the United States, Britain, the Philippines, and Mauritius, stabilised at about 3,500. Women, both military and civilian, became a permanent part of the island scene from 1982 and now comprise approaching 20 per cent of the residents, interestingly much the same proportion as in plantation days (and no doubt with some of the same consequences!).

The island saw a Royal Visit in November 1988 when HRH Prince Andrew, Duke of York, called at Diego Garcia on board the destroyer HMS *Edinburgh* in which he was a serving naval officer. He carried out a short official programme, including meeting both junior and senior members of the island community, planting a tree outside the British Representative's residence and visiting the Ship's Store to buy souvenirs. HRH Prince Edward was to follow in his brother's footsteps, visiting the island over two days in September 1992.

The year 1990 saw the 25th anniversary of the establishment of the British Indian Ocean Territory. This was marked by a number of events, including the grant of a Flag and a Coat of Arms with the appropriate motto 'In tutela nostra, Limuria' (Limuria is in our trust) by Her Majesty The Queen, the issue of commemorative stamps, and the launching of a fund to preserve as much as possible of the main buildings at the old East Point Plantation. There were celebrations on or near the actual anniversary of 8 November both in London and Diego Garcia. A reception was held in the Durbar Court of the Old India Office in London, which was attended by the Duke of York as well as a senior American delegation. On Diego Garcia itself there was a parade, tree-planting, athletic events and entertainment in which the whole island community participated. And Anniversary Island, the new islet at the mouth of the lagoon, was claimed and named.

The celebrations were held in a somewhat lower key than originally planned because of events in the Middle East. The facility on Diego Garcia played an important part in supporting the allied operation in the Gulf, Desert Shield, to counter the Iraqi aggression against Kuwait. Subsequently B52 aircraft of the 4300th Provisional Bombardment Wing, commanded by Colonel Terry Burke USAF were based on the island. Along with associated KC-10 and KC-135 tankers for air-refuelling, they played a major role in Operation Desert Storm. One of the USAF planes involved in operations sadly came down because of a technical fault just to the north of the island with the loss of three young officers, Captain Jeffrey Olson and First Lieutenants Jorge Agteaga and Eric Hedeen. A monument to them has been erected at Point Marianne cemetery.

It was indeed appropriate that as the Territory celebrated its quarter century of separate existence, Diego Garcia fulfilled the vision of the Anglo-American founding fathers of the 1966 defence agreement, as well as the name applied to it by its present American residents, the 'Footprint of Freedom'.

XV

'One of the Wonderful Phenomena of our Globe'[1]

The role played by the military facilities in Diego Garcia in the 1991 Gulf War confirmed the island's strategic importance. Even with the end of the Cold War, the world remains a dangerous and unstable place, and international and regional security is underpinned by the existence of the 'Footprint of Freedom'. The present pattern of life in Diego Garcia therefore seems set to continue for some time and BIOT is likely to celebrate the 50th anniversary of its existence in due course.

While no change in the political status of the Territory is foreseeable, Britain has made it clear to Mauritius, which maintains a claim to it, that she would be prepared to cede the Chagos when they are no longer needed for defence purposes. But whatever their future significance in military terms, it can safely be said that the Chagos Archipelago, including Diego Garcia, is bound to be of growing international environmental importance.

The remoteness of the islands and, ironically, the existence of the military facilities, have served to safeguard their delicate ecology. They have been spared the impact of mass tourism and factory fishing, the environmental banes which are despoiling more and more of the rest of the Indian Ocean. The degradation of reef systems elsewhere, as is regrettably happening even in the case of the Great Barrier Reef of Australia, will make the reefs of the Chagos Archipelago more and more precious. Recognition of this led to the formation in 1992 of a society dedicated to the protection and promotion of the islands' environment and history called The Friends of the Chagos.[2]

While the BIOT administration is aware of its environmental responsibility, it cannot be taken for granted that this would continue to be the case if the status of the islands were ever to change. Although the return of the descendants of the *Ilois* who worked the plantations is unlikely to be a realistic proposition, hotel developments and fishing facilities could all too easily be introduced without proper consideration. It should be a condition of any future change in their status that the Chagos be designated an international environmental reservation with proper protection from the impact of human short-sightedness and greed.

Otherwise, it might be better if Diego Garcia and its fellow Peaks of Limuria were to slip once more under the waters of the Indian Ocean.

Notes

Chapter I A Laurel on the Sea

1 J. A. Thompson, *Only the Sun Remembers*, Andrew Dakers, London, 1956, p. 151.

2 G. C. Bourne, *The Island of Diego Garcia of the Chagos Group, Proceedings of the Royal Geographical Society*, June 1880, p. 393.

3 J. A. Thompson, 'War to the Atol', *Military Honours*, Fortune, 1946, p. 5.

4 Charles Grant, *History of Mauritius*, London, 1801, p. 333.

5 Abbé de Rochon, *Voyage à Madagascar et aux Indes orientales*; an account of the archipelagos and sand banks between the Maldive Islands and the Isles of France and Bourbon; Paris, 1791.

Chapter II Takamakas, Turtles, Corals, Coconut Crabs, Shearwaters and Sharks

1 G. C. Bourne, *The Island of Diego Garcia of the Chagos Group, Proceedings of the Royal Geographical Society*, June 1880, p. 386.

2 Charles Pridham, *England's Colonial Empire: Mauritius and its Dependencies*, Smith, Elder, London, 1846, p. 402.

3 Bourne, op. cit., p. 392.

Chapter III From out the Azure Main

1 Alfred, Lord Tennyson, *In Memoriam*, canto 123, Edward Moxon, London, 1850.

2 Charles Darwin, *The Structure and Distribution of Coral Reefs*, Smith, Elder, London, 1842, p. 92.

3 Ibid. p. 1–2.

4 G. C. Bourne, *The Island of Diego Garcia of the Chagos Group, Proceedings of the Royal Geographical Society*, June 1880, p. 393.

Chapter IV Discovery

1 C. Maloney, *People of the Maldive Islands*, New Delhi, 1980, p. 113.

2 Statement of the Hon. Cecil Heftel, Congressional Record, 21 October 1977, and correspondence between the author and the Archivo General de Indies, Seville.

3 John S. Potter, *The Treasure Diver's Guide*, Robert Hale, London, 1973.

4 Sir James Lancaster, *The Voyages of Sir James Lancaster to Brazil and the East Indies 1591–1603*, edited by Sir William Foster, London, 1940.

5 Bombay Despatches, vol. 8, 3 May 1786, India Office Library Collection.

6 Archibald Blair, remarks and observations in a survey of the Chagos Archipelago, London 1788.

7 James Horsburgh, *Directions for Sailing to and from the East Indies*, Black, Parry and Kingsbury, London, 1809, p. 132.

Chapter V Settlement

1 Alexander Dalrymple, 'Memoir relative to the island of Diego Garcia', April 1787, MS National Library of Australia, Canberra.

2 Description from a map made by Captain Thomas Forrest and published by Dalrymple, London, 1786.

3 Letter from R. H. Boddam and Council (Political and Secret Department) to Richard Thomas Benjamin Price and John Richmond Smyth, 7 March 1786, India Office Library Collection.

4 Letter from R. Price and R. Smyth from Diego Garcia to the

Committee of Secrecy, Court of Directors, 24 August 1786, India Office Library Collection.

5   Letter from Court of Directors to Bombay Council (Political and Secret Department), 23 March 1787, India Office Library Collection.

6   Bombay Despatches August/November 1986, India Office Library Collection.

7   Letter from Mr Laurent Barbé to Captain General De Caen, quoted in Sir Robert Scott's *Limuria*, Oxford University Press, 1961, p. 98.

8   D'Unienville, *Statistique de l'Ile Maurice*, Paris, 1838, p. 185.

9   Information from Mr K. Dirkzwager. Letter to author 15 February 1990.

10 Information from US National Archives. Letter from Mr T. Lane More, 25 October 1990.

11 Sir Lowry Cole's despatch of 14 September 1826 to Lord Bathurst.

12 C. Pridham, *England's Colonial Empire: Mauritius and its Dependencies*, Smith, Elder, 1846, p. 403.

Chapter VI   Abolition of Slavery

1   Quoted in Sir Robert Scott's *Limuria*, Oxford University Press, 1961, p. 117.

2   Despatch No. 568 from Mauritius of William Nicolay to the Rt Hon J. Spring Rice MP, 16 February 1835, FCO records.

3   Letter of instructions to Special Justice C. Anderson from the Colonial Secretary, Port Louis, 13 June 1838, FCO records.

4   Special Justice C. Anderson's report to the Governor of Mauritius dated 5 September 1838, FCO records.

5   Ibid.

6   Letter to Special Justice Anderson from the Colonial Secretary, Port Louis, 19 October 1838, FCO records.

7   C. Pridham, *England's Colonial Empire: Mauritius and its Dependencies*, Smith, Elder, 1846, p. 403.

Chapter VII   The Oil Island

1   Special Commissioners' Lieutenant H. Berkeley and J. Caldwell's report to the Colonial Secretary, Port Louis, 25 June 1859, p. 12, FCO records.

2 Ibid.

3 Report of Special Magistrate E. Pakenham Brooks, 16 December 1875, FCO records.

4 G. C. Bourne, *The Island of Diego Garcia of the Chagos Group, Proceedings of the Royal Geographical Society,* June 1880, pp. 388–9.

Chapter VIII   The Coaling Station Interlude

1 Report No. 312 of Lionel Cox, Acting Procurator-General of Mauritius to the Acting Colonial Secretary, Port Louis, 27 March 1884, FCO records.

2 Report by Inspector of Police J. Shepherd, Port Louis, 20 February 1884, FCO records.

3 G. C. Bourne, *The Island of Diego Garcia of the Chagos Group, Proceedings of the Royal Geographical Society,* June 1880, pp. 389–90.

4 Report by Acting Magistrate Ivanoff Dupont, 22 December 1884, p. 920, FCO records.

5 Ibid., p. 926, FCO records.

6 Report by Lionel Cox, Acting Procurator-General of Mauritius, op. cit., FCO records.

7 Report of the Police and Stipendiary Magistrate A. Boucherat, Port Louis, 21 July 1888, FCO records.

Chapter IX   The Emden Incident

1 G. C. Bourne, *The Island of Diego Garcia of the Chagos Group, Proceedings of the Royal Geographical Society,* June 1880, p. 391.

2 Lt Franz Joseph, Prince of Hohenzollern, *My experiences in SMS Emden,* Herbert Jenkins, London, 1928, p. 132.

3 Ibid., p. 133.

4 Ibid., p. 136.

Chapter X   Partir C'est Mourir un Peu: Life between the Wars

1 C. Pridham, *England's Colonial Empire: Mauritius and its Dependencies,* Smith, Elder, London, 1846, pp. 402–3.

2   G. C. Bourne, *The Island of Diego Garcia of the Chagos Group, Proceedings of the Royal Geographical Society,* June 1880, p. 390.

3   Pridham, op. cit., p. 402–3.

4   Report of the Lord Bishop of Mauritius on his visitation to the Seychelles Islands and Chagos, Port Louis, 14 July 1859, FCO records.

5   Roger Dussercle, *Achipel de Chagos: en mission,* Port Louis, 1934.

6   Original research by the author in Mozambique.

7   Edmond Haraucourt: 'Rondel de l'Adieu', Seul, 1891.

Chapter XI   Outpost of Empire: Diego Garcia and the Second World War

1   J. A. Thompson, *Military Honours,* Fortune Press, London, 1946, p. 6.

2   J. A. Thompson, *Only the Sun Remembers,* Andrew Dakers, 1956, p. 151.

3   Ibid., p. 162.

4   Ibid., p. 176.

5   Ibid., pp. 180–3.

6   J. A. Thompson, *Military Honours,* p. 4.

7   Mr Fred Barnett's correspondence with the author, 1990.

8   Operations Record Book No. 205 Squadron RAF, Air Historical Branch, MOD, London.

9   Report of Mr Jollivet on his visit to Diego Garcia and Peros Banhos, March 1901, FCO records.

10 F. D. Ommanney, *The Shoals of Capricorn,* Longmans, Green and Co., London, 1952.

Chapter XII   The End of an Era

1   Sir Robert Scott, *Limuria,* Oxford University Press, 1961, p. 244.

2   Ibid., p. 248.

3   Ibid., p. 26.

Chapter XIII The Establishment of the British Indian Ocean Territory and the Coming of the Americans

1 G. C. Bourne, *The Island of Diego Garcia of the Chagos Group, Proceedings of the Royal Geographical Society,* June 1880, p. 391.

2 Statutory Instruments 1965, No. 1920: Overseas Territories: The British Indian Ocean Territory Order 1965.

3 Exchange of Notes concerning the availability for defence purposes of the British Indian Ocean Territory, London, 30 December 1966, Treaty Series No. 15 (1967) Cmnd 3231, HMSO.

Chapter XIV Footprint of Freedom

1 Letter from Commander Canter to the author, 19 November 1990.

2 Exchange of Notes concerning a United States Navy support facility on Diego Garcia, British Indian Ocean Territory, London, 25 February 1976, Cmnd 6413, HMSO.

3 Commander Canter's letter to the author, 16 January 1991.

Chapter XV 'One of the Wonderful Phenomena of our Globe'

1 James Horsburgh, *Directions for Sailing to and from the East Indies . . .* , London, 1809, 1826, p. 163.

2 Friends of the Chagos, c/o John Topp, 20 Lupus Street, London SW1V 3DZ. Telephone 0171 834 3079.

Bibliography

BELLAMY, David, *Half of Paradise*, Cassell, London, 1979

BENSON, Peter, *A Lesser Dependency*, Macmillan, London, 1989, Penguin, 1990

BOURNE, Gilbert C., *The Island of Diego Garcia of the Chagos Group, Proceedings of the Royal Geographical Society*, London, June 1880

BOXER, C. R., *The Portuguese Seaborne Empire*, Hutchinson, 1969

CHURCHILL, Winston S., *The World Crisis*, Thornton, Butterworth, London, 1923

—— *The Second World War*, Cassell, London, 1950

DARWIN, Charles, *The Structure and Distribution of Coral Reefs*, London, 1842

DUSSERCLE, Roger, *Archipel de Chagos: en mission*, General Printing and Stationery Co. Ltd., Port Louis, 1934, 1935

—— *L'Ile de d'Aigle: Noufrage de la Barque Diego*, General Printing and Stationery Co. Ltd., Port Louis, 1936

FREGOS, Paul, *Dreams of Empire*, Hutchinson, London, 1989

FRY, Howard T., *Alexander Dalrymple and the Expansion of British Trade*, Frank Cass, 1979

FULLER, Jack, *Paved Over Paradise*, Foreign Policy, 1977

GRANT, Charles, *History of Mauritius*, London, 1801

HARRISON, Kirby, *The Seabees at Work, Proceedings*, 1979

HOHENZOLLERN, Franz Joseph, *My Experiences in SMS Emden*, Herbert Jenkins, London, 1928

HORSBURGH, James, *Directions for Sailing to and from the East Indies . . . and Interadjacent Parts*, London, 1809, 1826

HUTSON, A. M., *Observation on the Birds of Diego Garcia, Chagos Archipelago, With Notes on Other Vertebrates*, The Smithsonian Institute, Washington DC, 1975

LANCASTER, Sir James, *The Voyages of Sir James Lancaster to Brazil and the East Indies 1591–1603*, ed. Sir William Foster, London, 1940

LEE, Jacques K., *Sega*, Nautilus, London, 1990

MALONEY, C. *People of the Maldive Islands*, New Delhi, 1980

OMMANNEY, F. D., *The Shoals of Capricorn*, Longmans, Green & Co, London, 1952

PHILLIMORE, R. H., *Historical Records of the Survey of India*, Vol. I, Survey of India, 1945

POTTER, John S., *The Treasure Diver's Guide*, Robert Hale and Co., London, 1973

PRIDHAM, C., *England's Colonial Empire: Mauritius and its Dependencies*, Smith, Elder, London, 1846

ROCHON, Abbé A. M. de, *Voyage à Madagascar et aux Indes orientales*, Paris, 1791

SCOTT, Robert, *Limuria*, Oxford University Press, 1961, and Greenwood Press, Westport, Conn, USA, 1974

SPRAY, William A., 'British Surveys in the Chagos Archipelago in the late 18th Century', *Mariner's Mirror*, January 1970

STODDART, D. R. and TAYLOR, *The Geography and Ecology of Diego Garcia*, The Smithsonian Institute, Washington DC, 1971

THOMPSON, J. Alan, *Only the Sun Remembers*, Andrew Dakers, London, 1956

—— *Military Honours*, Fortune Press, London, 1946

TOPP, J. M. W., *An Annotated Checklist of the Flora of Diego Garcia*, The Smithsonian Institute, Washington DC, 1988

TOUSSAINT, Auguste, *Histoire de l'Océan Indien*, Presses Universitaires de France, Paris, 1962

d'UNIENVILLE, M. C. A. M., *Statistique de L'Île Maurice et ses Dependances*, Gustav Barba, Paris, 1838

WALKER, Grazia, *Diego Garcia Atoll: Ecological Considerations*, University of Maryland, 1986

WINCHESTER, Simon, *Outposts*, Hodder and Stoughton, London, 1985 and Sceptre, 1981

Also original records, despatches and reports from the India Office Library, the Foreign & Commonwealth Office archives, the British Library and the Library of Congress.

Index

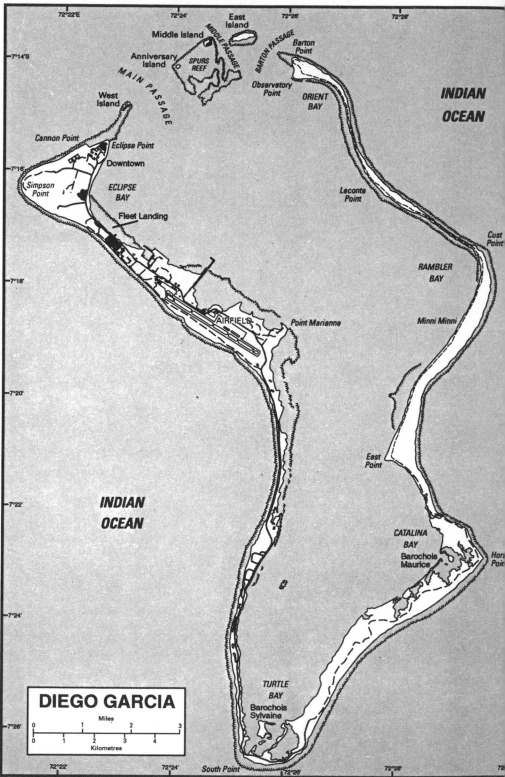

72°22'E · 72°24' · 72°26' · 72°26'

7°14'S

East
Island

Middle Island · MIDDLE PASSAGE

Anniversary
Island · SPURS
REEF

Barton
Point

BARTON PASSAGE

Observatory
Point

ORIENT
BAY

INDIAN
OCEAN

West
Island

MAIN PASSAGE

Cannon Point

Eclipse Point

Downtown

7°16'

Simpson
Point

ECLIPSE
BAY

Fleet Landing

Leconte
Point

Cust
Point

RAMBLER
BAY

7°18'

AIRFIELD

Point Marianne

Minni Minni

7°20'

INDIAN
OCEAN

East
Point

7°22'

CATALINA
BAY

Barochois
Maurice

Hor
Poir

7°24'

TURTLE
BAY

Barochois
Sylvaine

DIEGO GARCIA

Miles

0   1   2   3

0   1   2   3   4

Kilometres

7°26'

72°22' · 72°24' · South Point · 72°26' · 72°28' · 72

11826 (CAD) - July 1993 819/93

Foreign and Commonwealth Office Library Map Se